Gorgeous & Gruesome

CAKES FOR CHILDREN

Gorgeous & Gruesome
CAKES FOR CHILDREN
30 original and fun designs kids will love

DEBBIE BROWN

NEW
HOLLAND

For Hannah

First published in 2010 by New Holland Publishers (UK) Ltd
London • Cape Town • Sydney • Auckland
Garfield House, 86–88 Edgware Road, London W2 2EA, United Kingdom
www.newhollandpublishers.com

80 McKenzie Street, Cape Town 8001, South Africa
Unit 1, 66 Gibbes Street, Chatswood, NSW 2067, Australia
218 Lake Road, Northcote, Auckland

ISBN 978 1 84773 646 8

10 9 8 7 6 5 4 3 2 1

Editor: Amy Corstorphine
Design: AG&G Books
Photographs: Clive Streeter
Production: Laurence Poos
Editorial Direction: Rosemary Wilkinson

Reproduction by Pica Digital Pte Ltd, Singapore

Printed and bound in Malaysia by Times Offset (M) Sdn. Bhd.

For information on cake decorating workshops visit www.debbiebrownscakes.co.uk,
or email debra.brown@btinternet.com

Contents

Introduction

I really enjoyed writing this title with its fun mix of gorgeous and gruesome inspired designs for children. The gorgeous designs were easy to imagine, a little pink perhaps, a magical castle, a pretty fairy, some sparkle or a cute face and there's your appealing gorgeous cake that draws looks of admiration on the special day from all those little faces looking up at you.

When making some of the more gruesome designs, a colleague's words kept ringing in my ears, 'You couldn't make anything look ugly! Every piece of sugar you touch turns out cute!' I suppose it's rather true as most of the designs herein really aren't too gruesome at all. They are gruesome without being too much so – even the Ugly Bug has a funny facial expression that couldn't offend and the Monster instead of being angry just looks endearing!

I could've added some ghouls, a little blood and guts, perhaps an ugly worm or some disgusting looking rotting brains oozing out of the Pirate Skull's eye, or a pretty little butterfly sitting on the Baby Dinosaur's tongue about to be his tea, but decided to keep the designs slightly tamer, to stop those widened eyes of horror from little children's faces. I know they love the really gruesome ideas for cakes, but when it comes to the serving, the wrinkling of noses is common and they never really want to consume the really unsavoury looking ones, and it's such a waste of a nice celebration cake and all the time you've spent perfecting it.

I hope you find something to inspire you within these pages and the designs give you and the lucky recipients much pleasure. I've been writing and designing for many years and all of these cakes are achievable within a sensible timeframe although I recommend you leave plenty of time to decorate to alleviate any stress as the special day nears. I've found as long as the cake is sealed tightly with a good covering of sugarpaste no later than a day after baking then it can, depending on the climate you are working in, last anything up to a week before consumption, allowing you time to perfect your masterpiece. Just have fun and be happy to have found this wonderful and rewarding pastime.

Debbie

Basic recipes

Butter sponge cake

This recipe is rich and moist but with the addition of a little extra flour makes it slightly denser so perfect for sculpting. I would recommend using this recipe in preference to shop bought sponge mixes as these are often too soft and crumbly to withstand being sculpted into different shapes.

If you have a fan assisted oven, it may be advisable to reduce the suggested oven temperature slightly. I also recommend placing a metal baking (cookie) sheet onto the top of the bakeware so the cake is protected from the hot air during baking.

1 Preheat the oven to 150°C/300°F/Gas Mark 2-3. Grease and line the bakeware. Sift the flour into a bowl.

2 Soften the butter and place into the food processor or a large mixing bowl. Sift and add the caster (superfine) sugar. Beat until the mixture becomes lighter in colour with a fluffy texture.

3 Add the eggs along with two thirds of the flour and beat well.

4 Add the Vanilla essence/flavouring and then fold in the remaining flour.

5 Spoon the mixture into the bakeware and level the top.

6 Bake in the centre of the oven until a skewer inserted into the centre comes out clean.

7 When baked, remove from the oven and leave to cool for five minutes before turning out onto a wire rack to cool completely. When cold, store in an airtight container or double wrap in clingfilm (plastic wrap) for at least eight hours, allowing the texture to settle before use.

	Bakeware	Caster (superfine) sugar (sifted)	Unsalted butter, softened	Large eggs	Self-raising flour (sifted)	Vanilla essence (extract)	Baking time
Princess castle	3 x 15 cm (6 in) round tins	340g (12 oz/1¾c)	340g (12oz/1½c)	6	430g (15oz/3½c)	1 tsp	1–1¼ hours
Ted in a box	2 x 15 cm (6 in) square tins and 2 x 11 cm (4½ in) ovenproof bowls or tins	450g (1lb/2⅓c)	450g (1lb/2c)	8	565g (1lb 4oz/4½c)	1 tsp	1–1¼ hours
Sea palace	1 x 18 cm (7 in) and 2 x 15 cm (6 in) round tins	400g (14oz/2c)	400g (14oz/1¾c)	7	500g (1lb 1¾oz/4c)	1 tsp	1–1¼ hours
Dotty dog and Alien spaceship	1 x 15 cm (6 in) and 1 x 20 cm (8 in) dia. ovenproof bowls or dome-shaped tins	400g (14oz/2c)	400g (14oz/1¾c)	7	500g (1lb 1¾oz/4c)	1 tsp	1¼–1½ hours
Swamp monster	1 x 23 cm (9 in) dia. ovenproof bowl or dome-shaped tin	340g (12oz/1¾c)	340g (12oz/1½c)	6	430g (15oz/3½c)	1 tsp	1½–2 hours
Spider trap	3 x 15 cm (6 in) square tins	450g (1lb/2⅓c)	450g (1lb/2c)	8	565g (1lb 4oz/4½c)	1 tsp	1¼–1½ hours
Alien egg and Ugly bug	2 x 15 cm (6 in) dia. ovenproof bowls or dome-shaped tins	340 g (12oz/1¾c)	340g (12oz/1½c)	6	430g (15oz/3½c)	1 tsp	1¼–1½ hours
Frog prince	1 x 20 cm (8 in) dia. ovenproof bowl or dome-shaped tin and 1 x 20 cm (8 in) round tin	450g (1lb/2⅓c)	450g (1lb/2c)	8	565g (1lb 4oz/4½c)	1 tsp	1¼–1½ hours
Scary octopus	2 x 22 cm (9 in) dia. ovenproof bowls or dome-shaped tins	340g (12oz/1¾c)	340g (12oz/1½c)	6	430g (15oz/3½c)	½ tsp	1–1¼ hours
Bugs	12 x 7-8 cm (2½-3 in) ovenproof bowls or dome-shaped tins	115g (4oz/⅔c)	115g (4oz/½c)	2	145g (5oz/1¼c)	½ tsp	20–30 minutes
Crowns and tiaras	12-hole bun tin	115g (4oz/⅔c)	115g (4 oz/½c)	2	145g (5oz/1¼c)		20–30 minutes
Midnight fairies and Worms	10 cm (4 in) & 20 cm (8 in) round tins	340g (12oz/1¾c)	340g (12oz/1½c)	6	430g (15oz/3½c)	1 tsp	1–¼ hours
Ragdoll	2 x 15 cm (6 in) square tins and 2 x 8 cm (3 in) ovenproof bowls or dome-shaped tins	340g (12oz/1¾c)	340g (12oz/1½c)	6	430g (15oz/3½c)	1 tsp	15–20 minutes small bowls, 1 hour square tins/pans
Cloud castle	28 x 7-8 cm (2½-3 in) ovenproof bowls or dome-shaped tins	225g (8oz/1c+2 Tbsp)	225g (8 oz/1c)	4	285g (10oz/2¼c)	1 tsp	20–30 minutes
Glass slipper	25 cm (10 in) round cake tin	340g (12oz/1¾c)	340g (12oz/1½c)	6	430g (15oz/3½c)	1 tsp	1 hour

	Bakeware	Caster (superfine) sugar (sifted)	Unsalted butter, softened	Large eggs	Self-raising flour (sifted)	Vanilla essence (extract)	Baking time
Pirate skull	2 x 15 cm (6 in) round cake tins and 1 x 15 cm (6 in) dia. ovenproof bowl or dome-shaped tin	285g (10oz/1½c)	285g (10oz/1¼c)	5	340g (12oz/2¾c)	1 tsp	1–1¼ hours
Shark!	1 x 20 cm (8 in) round tin and 1 x 20 cm (8 in) diameter ovenproof bowl or dome-shaped tin	340g (12oz/1¾c)	340g (12oz/1½c)	6	430g (15oz/3½c)	1 tsp	1¼–1½ hours
Eyeballs	1 x 15 cm (6 in) & 1 x 10 cm (4 in) square tins	285g (10oz/1½c)	285g (10oz/1¼c)	5	340g (12oz/2¾c)	1 tsp	50 minutes –1 hour
Fairy wand	1 x 30 cm (12 in) square cake tin	450g (1lb/2¼c)	450g (1lb/2c)	8	565g (1lb 4oz/4½c)	1 tsp	1–1¼ hours
Flower fairy	1 x 15 cm (6 in) and 2 x 10 cm (4 in) round cake tins	340g (12oz/1¾c)	340g (12oz/1½c)	6	430g (15oz/3½c)	1 tsp	1–1¼ hours
Trumpet tower	2 x 15 cm (6 in) and 2 x 10 cm (4 in) round cake tins	400g (14oz/2c)	400g (14oz/1¾c)	7	500g (1lb 1¾oz/4c)	1 tsp	1–1¼ hours
Hey monster!	2 x 15 cm (6 in) round cake tins and 1 x 15 cm (6 in) dia. ovenproof bowl or dome-shaped cake tin	400g (14oz/2c)	400g (14oz/1¾c)	7	500g (1lb 1¾oz/4c)	1 tsp	1–1¼ hours
The dungeon	2 x 18 cm (7 in) square cake tins	400g (14oz/2c)	400g (14oz/1¾c)	7	500g (1lb 1¾oz/4c)	1 tsp	1¼–1½ hours
Troll house	1 x 20 cm (8 in) square cake tin	225g (8oz/1c+2 Tbsp)	225g (8oz/1c)	4	285g (10oz/2¼c)	1 tsp	1–1¼ hours
Acorn fairy	1 x 20 cm (8 in) & 1 x 15 cm (6 in) round cake tins	400g (14oz/2c)	400g (14oz/1¾c)	7	500g (1lb 1¾oz/4c)	1 tsp	1–1½ hours
The butterfly ball	1 x 20 cm (8 in) round cake tin	225g (8oz/1c+2 Tbsp)	225g (8 oz/1c)	4	285g (10oz/2¼c)	1 tsp	1¼–1½ hours
Baby dinosaur	1 x 20 cm (8 in) round cake tin, 1 x 20 cm (8 in) & 2 x 12 cm (5 in) ovenproof bowls or dome-shaped cake tins	400g (14oz/2c)	400g (14oz/1¾c)	7	500g (1lb 1¾oz/4c)	1 tsp	30–50 minutes

Pretty pink raspberry cake

This recipe is gorgeously pretty pink in colour and tastes great with the addition of the raspberry jelly (Jell-O). The jelly also helps to slightly firm the texture of the cake, making it perfect for sculptures.

If you have a fan-assisted oven, it may be advisable to reduce the suggested oven temperature slightly. I also recommend placing a metal baking (cookie) sheet onto the top of the bakeware so the cake is protected from the hot air during baking.

1 Preheat the oven to 150°C/300°F/Gas Mark 2-3. Grease and line the bakeware. Sift the flour into a bowl.

2 Melt the jelly (Jell-O) for one minute in a microwave and then stir until dissolved.

3 Soften the butter and place into the food processor or a large mixing bowl. Sift and add the caster (superfine) sugar. Beat until the mixture becomes lighter in colour with a fluffy texture.

4 Add the eggs along with two thirds of the flour and beat well.

5 Add the melted jelly (Jell-O) and then fold in the remaining flour.

6 Spoon the mixture into the bakeware and level the top.

7 Bake in the centre of the oven until a skewer inserted into the centre comes out clean.

8 When baked, remove from the oven and leave to cool for five minutes before turning out onto a wire rack to cool completely. When cold, store in an airtight container or double wrap in clingfilm (plastic wrap) for at least eight hours, allowing the texture to settle before use.

	Bakeware	Caster (superfine) sugar (sifted)	Unsalted butter, softened	Large eggs	Self-raising flour (sifted)	Raspberry jelly (Jell-O)	Baking time
Princess castle	3 x 15 cm (6 in) round tins	340g (12oz/1¾c)	340g (12oz/1½c)	6	430g (15oz/3½c)	270g (9½oz/1¼c)	1–1¼ hours
Ted in a box	2 x 15 cm (6 in) square tins and 2 x 11 cm (4½ in) ovenproof bowls or tins	450g (1lb/2¼c)	450g (1lb/2c)	8	565g (1lb 4oz/4½c)	360g (12½oz /1²/₃c)	1–1¼ hours
Sea palace	1 x 18 cm (7 in) and 2 x 15 cm (6 in) round tins	400g (14oz/2c)	400g (14oz/1¾c)	7	500g (1lb 1¾oz/4c)	315g (11oz/1½c)	1–1¼ hours
Dotty dog and Alien spaceship	1 x 15 cm (6 in) and 1 x 20 cm (8 in) dia. ovenproof bowls or dome-shaped tins	400g (14oz/2c)	400g (14oz/1¾c)	7	500g (1lb 1¾oz/4c)	315g (11oz/1½c)	1¼–1½ hours
Swamp monster	1 x 23 cm (9 in) dia. ovenproof bowl or dome-shaped tin	340g (12oz/1¾c)	340g (12oz/1½c)	6	430g (15oz/3½c)	270g (9½oz/1¼c)	1½–2 hours
Spider trap	3 x 15 cm (6 in) square tins	450g (1lb/2¼c)	450 g (1lb/2c)	8	565g (1lb 4 oz/4½c)	360g (12½oz /1²/₃c)	1¼–1½ hours
Alien egg and Ugly bug	2 x 15 cm (6 in) dia. ovenproof bowls or dome-shaped tins	340g (12oz/1¾c)	340g (12oz/1½c)	6	430g (15oz/3½c)	270g (9½oz/1¼c)	1¼–1½ hours
Frog prince	1 x 20 cm (8 in) dia. ovenproof bowl or dome-shaped tin and 1 x 20 cm (8 in) round tin	450g (1lb/2¼c)	450g (1lb/2c)	8	565g (1lb 4 oz/4½c)	360g (12½oz /1²/₃c)	1¼–1½ hours
Scary octopus	2 x 22 cm (9 in) dia. ovenproof bowls or dome-shaped tins	340g (12oz/1¾c)	340g (12oz/1½c)	6	430g (15oz/3½c)	270g (9½oz/1¼c)	1–1¼ hours

	Bakeware	Caster (superfine) sugar (sifted)	Unsalted butter, softened	Large eggs	Self-raising flour (sifted)	Raspberry jelly (Jell-O)	Baking time
Bugs	12 x 7-8 cm (2½ - 3 in) ovenproof bowls or dome-shaped tins	115g (4oz/²/₃c)	115g (4 oz/½c)	2	145g (5oz/1¼c)	90g (3oz/¹/₃c)	20–30 minutes
Crowns and tiaras	12-hole bun tin	115g (4oz/²/₃c)	115g (4oz/½c)	2	145g (5oz/1¼c)	90g (3oz/¹/₃c)	20–30 minutes
Midnight fairies and Worms	10 cm (4 in) & 20 cm (8 in) round tins	340 g (12 oz/1¾c)	340g (12oz/ 1½c)	6	430g (15oz/3½c)	90g (3oz/¹/₃c)	1–¼ hours
Ragdoll	2 x 15 cm (6 in) square tins and 2 x 8 cm (3 in) ovenproof bowls or dome-shaped tins	340g (12oz/1¾c)	340g (12oz/1½c)	6	430g (15oz/3½c)	270g (9½oz/1¼c)	15–20 minutes small bowls, 1 hour square tins/ pans
Cloud castle	28 x 7-8 cm (2½-3 in) ovenproof bowls or dome-shaped tins	225g (8oz/ 1c+2 Tbsp)	225g (8 oz/1c)	4	285g (10oz/2¼c)	270g (9½oz/1¼c)	20–30 minutes
Glass slipper	25 cm (10 in) round cake tin	340g (12oz/1¾c)	340g (12oz/ 1½c)	6	430g (15oz/3½c)	180g (6¼ oz/¾c)	1 hour
Pirate skull	2 x 15 cm (6 in) round cake tins and 1 x 15 cm (6 in) dia. ovenproof bowl or dome-shaped tin	285g (10oz/1½c)	285g (10oz/1¼c)	5	340g (12oz/2¾c)	270g (9½oz/1¼c)	1–1¼ hours
Shark!	1 x 20 cm (8 in) round tin and 1 x 20 cm (8 in) diameter ovenproof bowl or dome-shaped tin	340g (12oz/1¾c)	340g (12oz/1½c)	6	430g (15 oz/3½c)	225g (8oz)	1¼–1½ hours
Eyeballs	1 x 15 cm (6 in) & 1 x 10 cm (4 in) square tins	285 g (10 oz/1½c)	285 g (10oz/1¼c)	5	340g (12oz/2¾c)	270g (9½oz/1¼c)	50 minutes –1 hour
Fairy wand	1 x 30 cm (12 in) square cake tin	450g (1lb/2¼c)	450g (1lb/2c)	8	565g (1lb 4oz/4½c)	225g (8oz/1c)	1–1¼ hours
Flower fairy	1 x 15 cm (6 in) and 2 x 10 cm (4 in) round cake tins	340g (12oz/1¾c)	340g (12oz/1½c)	6	430g (15oz/3½c)	360g (12½oz /1²/₃c)	1–1¼ hours
Trumpet tower	2 x 15 cm (6 in) and 2 x 10 cm (4 in) round cake tins	400g (14oz/2c)	400g (14oz/1¾c)	7	500g (1lb 1¾oz/4c)	270g (9½oz/1¼c)	1–1¼ hours
Hey monster!	2 x 15 cm (6 in) round cake tins and 1 x 15 cm (6 in) dia. ovenproof bowl or dome-shaped cake tin	400g (14oz/2c)	400g (14oz/1¾c)	7	500g (1lb 1¾oz/4c)	315g (11oz/1½c)	1–1¼ hours
The dungeon	2 x 18 cm (7 in) square cake tins	400g (14oz/2c)	400g (14oz/1¾c)	7	500g (1lb 1¾oz/4c)	315g (11oz/1½c)	1¼–1½ hours

	Bakeware	Caster (superfine) sugar (sifted)	Unsalted butter, softened	Large eggs	Self-raising flour (sifted)	Raspberry jelly (Jell-O)	Baking time
Troll house	1 x 20 cm (8 in) square cake tin	225g (8 oz/ 1c+2 Tbsp)	225g (8oz/1c)	4	285g (10oz/2¼c)	315g (11oz/1½c)	1–1¼ hours
Acorn fairy	1 x 20 cm (8 in) & 1 x 15 cm (6 in) round cake tins	400g (14 oz/2c)	400g (14oz/1¾c)	7	500g (1lb 1¾oz/4c)	315g (11oz/1½c)	1–1½ hours
The butterfly ball	1 x 20 cm (8 in) round cake tin	225g (8 oz/ 1c+2 Tbsp)	225g (8 oz/1c)	4	285g (10 oz/2¼c)	180g (6¼oz/¾c)	1¼–1½ hours
Baby dinosaur	1 x 20 cm (8 in) round cake tin, 1 x 20 cm (8 in) & 2 x 12 cm (5 in) ovenproof bowls or dome-shaped cake tins	400g (14oz/2c)	400g (14oz/1¾c)	7	500g (1lb 1¾oz/4c)	315g (11oz/1½c)	30–50 minutes

Slime lime cake

This recipe is gorgeously gruesome green in colour but tastes great with the flavour of the lime jelly (Jell-O). As the raw green jelly (Jell-O) is quite pale, I added a few small drops of liquid green food colouring into the cake mixture as this helps to intensify the colour, but of course you could leave this out if you wish.

If you have a fan assisted oven, it may be advisable to reduce the suggested oven temperature slightly. I also recommend placing a metal baking (cookie) sheet onto the top of the bakeware so the cake is protected from the hot air during baking.

1 Preheat the oven to 150°C/300°F/Gas Mark 2-3. Grease and line the bakeware. Sift the flour into a bowl.

2 Melt the jelly in a pan over a low heat or heat for one minute in a microwave and then stir until dissolved. Set aside to cool slightly.

3 Soften the butter and place into the food processor or a large mixing bowl. Sift and add the caster (superfine) sugar. Beat until the mixture becomes lighter in colour with a fluffy texture.

4 Add the eggs along with two thirds of the flour and beat well.

5 Add the melted jelly and the liquid food colouring if required. Fold in the remaining flour.

6 Spoon the mixture into the bakeware and level the top.

7 Bake in the centre of the oven until a skewer inserted into the centre comes out clean.

8 When baked, remove from the oven and leave to cool for five minutes before turning out onto a wire rack to cool completely. When cold, store in an airtight container or double wrap in clingfilm (plastic wrap) for at least eight hours, allowing the texture to settle before use.

	Bakeware	Caster (superfine) sugar (sifted)	Unsalted butter, softened	Large eggs	Self-raising flour (sifted)	Lime jelly (Jell-O)	Baking time
Princess castle	3 x 15 cm (6 in) round tins	340g (12oz/1¾c)	340g (12oz/1½c)	6	430g (15oz/3½c)	270g (9½oz/1¼c)	1–1¼ hours
Ted in a box	2 x 15 cm (6 in) square tins and 2 x 11 cm (4½ in) ovenproof bowls or tins	450g (1lb/2¼c)	450g (1lb/2c)	8	565g (1lb 4 oz/4½c)	360g (12½oz /1²/₃c)	1–1¼ hours
Sea palace	1 x 18 cm (7 in) and 2 x 15 cm (6 in) round tins	400g (14oz/2c)	400g (14oz/1¾c)	7	500g (1lb 1¾oz/4c)	315g (11oz/1½c)	1–1¼ hours
Dotty dog and Alien spaceship	1 x 15 cm (6 in) and 1 x 20 cm (8 in) dia. ovenproof bowls or dome-shaped tins	400g (14oz/2c)	400g (14oz/1¾c)	7	500g (1lb 1¾oz/4c)	315g (11oz/1½c)	1¼–1½ hours
Swamp monster	1 x 23 cm (9 in) dia. ovenproof bowl or dome-shaped tin	340g (12oz/1¾c)	340g (12oz/1½c)	6	430g (15oz/3½c)	270g (9½oz/1¼c)	1½–2 hours
Spider trap	3 x 15 cm (6 in) square tins	450g (1lb/2¼c)	450g (1lb/2c)	8	565g (1lb 4 oz/4½c)	360g (12½oz /1²/₃c)	1¼ –1½ hours
Alien egg and Ugly bug	2 x 15 cm (6 in) dia. ovenproof bowls or dome-shaped tins	340g (12oz/1¾c)	340g (12oz/1½c)	6	430g (15 oz/3½c)	270 g (9½oz/1¼c)	1¼–1½ hours
Frog prince	1 x 20 cm (8 in) dia. ovenproof bowl or dome-shaped tin and 1 x 20 cm (8 in) round tin	450g (1lb/2¼c)	450g (1lb/2c)	8	565g (1lb 4 oz/4½c)	360g (12½oz /1²/₃c)	1¼ –1½ hours
Scary octopus	2 x 22 crn (9 in) dia. ovenproof bowls or dome-shaped tins	340g (12oz/1¾c)	340g (12oz/1½c)	6	430g (15 oz/3½c)	270 g (9½oz/1¼c)	1–1¼ hours
Bugs	12 x 7-8 cm (2½ - 3 in) ovenproof bowls or dome-shaped tins	115g (4oz/²/₃c)	115g (4 oz/½c)	2	145g (5oz/1¼c)	90 g (3 oz/¹/₃c)	20–30 minutes
Crowns and tiaras	12-hole bun tin	115g (4oz/²/₃c)	115g (4oz/½c)	2	145g (5oz/1¼c)	90 g (3 oz/¹/₃c)	20–30 minutes
Midnight fairies and Worms	10 cm (4 in) & 20 cm (8 in) round tins	340g (12oz/1¾c)	340g (12oz/1½c)	6	430g (15 oz/3½c)	270 g (9½oz/1¼c)	1– ¼ hours
Ragdoll	2 x 15 cm (6 in) square tins and 2 x 8 cm (3 in) ovenproof bowls or dome-shaped tins	340g (12oz/1¾c)	340g (12oz/1½c)	6	430g (15oz/3½c)	270 g (9½oz/1¼c)	15–20 minutes small bowls, 1 hour square tins/ pans
Cloud castle	28 x 7-8 cm (2½-3 in) ovenproof bowls or dome-shaped tins	225g (8oz/ 1c+2 Tbsp)	225g (8oz/1c)	4	285g (10 oz/2¼c)	180g (6¼ oz/¾c)	20–30 minutes
Glass slipper	25 cm (10 in) round cake tin	340g (12oz/1¾c)	340g (12oz/1½c)	6	430g (15oz/3½c)	270 g (9½oz/1¼c)	1 hour

	Bakeware	Caster (superfine) sugar (sifted)	Unsalted butter, softened	Large eggs	Self-raising flour (sifted)	Lime jelly (Jell-O)	Baking time
Pirate skull	2 x 15 cm (6 in) round cake tins and 1 x 15 cm (6 in) dia. ovenproof bowl or dome-shaped tin	285g (10oz/1½c)	285g (10oz/1¼c)	5	340g (12oz/2¾c)	225g (8oz/1c)	1–1¼ hours
Shark!	1 x 20 cm (8 in) round tin and 1 x 20 cm (8 in) diameter ovenproof bowl or dome-shaped tin	340g (12 oz/1¾c)	340g (12oz/1½c)	6	430g (15oz/3½c)	270g (9½oz/1¼c)	1¼–1½ hours
Eyeballs	1 x 15 cm (6 in) & 1 x 10 cm (4 in) square tins	285g (10oz/1½c)	285g (10oz/1¼c)	5	340g (12oz/2¾c)	225g (8oz/1c)	50 minutes –1 hour
Fairy wand	1 x 30 cm (12 in) square cake tin	450g (1lb/2¼c)	450g (1lb/2c)	8	565g (1lb 4 oz/4½c)	360g (12½oz /1²/₃c)	1–1¼ hours
Flower fairy	1 x 15 cm (6 in) and 2 x 10 cm (4 in) round cake tins	340g (12oz/1¾c)	340g (12oz/ 1½c)	6	430g (15 oz/3½c)	270g (9½oz/1¼c)	1–1¼ hours
Trumpet tower	2 x 15 cm (6 in) and 2 x 10 cm (4 in) round cake tins	400g (14oz/2c)	400g (14oz/1¾c)	7	500g (1lb 1¾oz/4c)	315g (11oz/1½c)	1–1¼ hours
Hey monster!	2 x 15 cm (6 in) round cake tins (pans) and 1 x 15 cm (6 in) dia. ovenproof bowl or dome-shaped cake tin	400g (14oz/2c)	400g (14oz/1¾c)	7	500g (1lb 1¾oz/4c)	315g (11oz/1½c)	1–1¼ hours
The dungeon	2 x 18 cm (7 in) square cake tins	400g (14oz/2c)	400g (14oz/1¾c)	7	500g (1lb 1¾oz/4c)	315g (11oz/1½c)	1¼–1½ hours
Troll house	1 x 20 cm (8 in) square cake tin	225g (8oz/ 1c+2 Tbsp)	225g (8oz/1c)	4	285g (10oz/2¼c)	180g (6¼oz/¾c)	1–1¼ hours
Acorn fairy	1 x 20 cm (8 in) & 1 x 15 cm (6 in) round cake tins	400g (14oz/2c)	400g (14oz/1¾c)	7	500g (1lb 1¾oz/4c)	315 g (11oz/1½c)	1–1½ hours
The butterfly ball	1 x 20 cm (8 in) round cake tin	225g (8oz/ 1c+2 Tbsp)	225g (8oz/1c)	4	285g (10oz/2¼c)	180g (6¼oz/¾c)	1¼–1½ hours
Baby dinosaur	1 x 20 cm (8 in) round cake tin, 1 x 20 cm (8 in) & 2 x 12 cm (5 in) ovenproof bowls or dome-shaped cake tins	400g (14oz/2c)	400g (14oz/1¾c)	7	500g (1lb 1¾oz/4c)	315g (11oz/1½c)	30–50 minutes

14

SUGAR SYRUP

Sugar syrup is an easy way to ensure your cake remains moist during the preparation process and of course the serving. When preparing your cake, brush or dab sugar syrup carefully over each sponge cake layer, preferably with a silicone pastry brush and before the cake filling is added. The syrup slowly soaks into the sponge until it is distributed evenly throughout the cake. I also brush syrup over the top and sides of the sponge cake just before the crumb-coat is spread over the surface as I find it spreads a little easier.

Some cake decorators prefer to be generous when brushing on the syrup whilst others are more conservative. I find excessive sugar syrup can cause the sponge to become very sweet, so I recommend the following quantity. You can, of course, add more; in fact, many cake decorators use double these quantities.

- 115g (4oz) caster (superfine) sugar
- 125ml (4fl oz) water
- 5ml (1tsp) flavouring (optional)

1 Pour the measured sugar into a saucepan along with the water. Heat gently and bring to the boil, stirring carefully. Simmer for one minute to ensure all sugar granules have completely dissolved. Do not leave unattended as sugar can burn easily. Remove from the heat and set aside to cool.

2 Store in an airtight container and refrigerate. Use within one month.

3 Flavouring sugar syrup is not absolutely necessary but if you've baked a flavoured sponge cake then flavouring the sugar syrup to complement it can really enhance the taste. Although the most popular flavouring is vanilla, different seedless fruit jams also work very well.

BUTTERCREAM

A great versatile filling and the first choice for many, buttercream made with real unsalted butter is delicious. Can be carefully flavoured for choice. This amount is enough for each project in the book, plus a little extra just in case.

Makes approximately 625g (1¼lb/3¾c).
- 175g (6oz/¾c) unsalted butter, softened
- 2–3 tbsp milk
- 1 tsp flavouring (optional)

- 450g (1lb/3¼c) icing (powdered) sugar, sifted

1 Place the softened butter, milk and flavouring into a mixer. Mix on medium speed and add the icing (powdered) sugar a little at a time. Mix until light, fluffy and pale in colour.

2 Store in an airtight container and use within 10 days. Bring to room temperature and beat again before use.

BUTTERCREAM VARIATIONS

Chocolate
Fold in 145g–200g (5–7oz) of melted and cooled dark, milk or white chocolate

Orange or lemon
Add 30–45ml (2–3 level tbsp) of orange or lemon curd.

Raspberry
Add 30–45ml (2–3 level tbsp) of seedless raspberry jam.

Lime
Add 30–45ml (2–3 level tbsp) of freshly squeezed lime juice.

GANACHE

Ganache is a rich chocolate filling and coating, popular with cake decorators as it's not only a delicious filling, but when spread on the surface of the cake as a crumb coat smoothes the surface ready for a neat application of sugarpaste (rolled fondant). Although not absolutely necessary, I recommend you leave the ganache covered cake to set for 24 hours room temperature. This allows the surface to set hard, making it easier to gain great results. To ensure the ganache sets firm enough to stabilize the cake and make it easier to

cover, the cream quantity differs for each recipe due to the higher fat content of both milk and white chocolate. Although both will set well, dark ganache will set the hardest. In warmer climates you may slightly reduce the cream quantity further.

When you're ready to apply the sugarpaste, the surface needs either a little sugar syrup, jam or softened ganache stippled over the surface to make it sticky ready for the covering. Take care not to add too much moisture otherwise your sugarpaste covering may slip.

This amount is enough for each project in the book, plus a little extra just in case.

Dark Chocolate Ganache
- 625g (1lb 6oz) dark couverture chocolate
- 500ml (18fl oz) fresh single or whipping cream

Milk Chocolate Ganache
- 625g (1lb 6oz) milk couverture chocolate
- 340ml (12fl oz) fresh single or whipping cream

White Chocolate Ganache
- 625g (1lb 6oz) milk or white couverture chocolate
- 170ml (6fl oz) fresh single or whipping cream

1 Melt the chocolate in a bowl over a pan of hot water (or a bain-marie) to 40°C (105°F).

2 Put the cream in a saucepan and bring to a simmer for a minute. Allow to cool slightly.

3 Using a hand whisk, slowly pour the cream over the melted chocolate whisking gently together. Don't be

alarmed if the mixture thickens quickly, keep whisking until combined.

4 Allow the Ganache to cool, then transfer into an airtight container and refrigerate. Use within one week.

SUGARPASTE

Good quality ready-made sugarpaste is easy to use, produces great results and comes in a range of colours. Sugarpaste is widely available in the UK and many other countries around the world through cake decorating outlets and some supermarkets. There are many brands to choose from so it is best to try out as many as you can to find out which works for you best.

If you find ready-made sugarpaste difficult to source, here is a simple recipe:

Makes 625 g (1¼ lb/3¾c)

- 1 egg white made up from dried egg albumen
- 2 tbsp liquid glucose
- 625g (1¼ lb/4½c) icing (powdered) sugar
- A little white vegetable fat (shortening) if required
- A pinch of CMC or Gum Tragacanth if required

1 Put the egg white mixture and liquid glucose into a bowl, using a warm spoon for the liquid glucose.

2 Sift the icing (powdered) sugar into the bowl, adding a little at a time and stirring until the mixture thickens.

3 Turn out onto a work surface dusted liberally with icing (powdered) sugar and knead the paste until soft, smooth and pliable. If the paste is a little dry and cracked, fold in a little vegetable fat and knead again. If the paste is very soft and sticky, add a little more icing (powdered) sugar or to stabilise further a pinch of CMC or Gum Tragacanth.

4 Put immediately into a polythene bag and store in an airtight container. Keep cool at room temperature, or refridgerate. Bring back to room temperature and knead thoroughly before use. Can be frozen for up to 3 months.

ROYAL ICING

Royal icing is used to pipe details, e.g., hair, fur effect, etc. I also use royal icing to stick items together, as when it dries it will hold items firmly in place. Ready-made royal icing can be obtained from supermarkets or in powder form to which you only have to add water (follow instructions on the packet). If you prefer to make your own, follow this recipe.

Makes 75g (2½ oz)

- 1 level tsp egg albumen
- 3 tsp water
- 65–70g (2¼oz/½c) icing (powdered) sugar

Put the egg albumen into a bowl. Add the water and stir until dissolved. Beat in the icing (powdered) sugar a little at a time until the icing if firm, glossy and forms peaks if a spoon is pulled out.

To stop the icing forming a crust, place a damp cloth over the top of the bowl until you are ready to use it or transfer to an airtight container and refrigerate.

EDIBLE GLUE

This recipe makes a strong edible glue which works extremely well. Alternatively, readymade edible glue can be purchased from specialist cake decorating outlets.

- One large pinch of CMC powder
- 2 tbsp boiled water, cooled until warm

1 Mix powder with warm water and leave to stand until powder is fully absorbed. The glue should be smooth and have a soft dropping consistency. If the glue thickens after a few days, add a few drops more water. Store airtight in the refrigerator and use within 1–2 weeks.

NOTE: CMC is an abbreviation of CARBOXYMETHYL CELLULOSE, an edible thickener widely used in the food industry. Must be food grade C1000P/E466. Use Gum Tragacanth as an alternative.

MODELLING PASTE RECIPE

This quick and easy recipe makes a high quality modelling paste.

- 450 g (1 lb) sugarpaste (see page 15)
- 1–2 level tsp CMC powder

1 Knead CMC into sugarpaste. The sugarpaste starts to thicken as soon as CMC is incorporated so can be used immediately. More thickening will happen gradually over a period of 24 hours. Amount of CMC can be varied depending on usage and atmospheric conditions. Store airtight.

QUICK PASTILLAGE RECIPE

Pastillage is fast drying, suitable for freestanding items like cards, boxes, etc., as the paste dries extremely hard and will keep shape.

Makes 260 g (9 oz) pastillage

- 2 tsp CMC powder or gum tragacanth
- 260 g (9 oz) royal icing

1 Mix 2 level tsp of CMC into 260 g (9 oz) stiff peak royal icing. The mixture will thicken immediately. Knead on a work surface sprinkled liberally with icing (powdered) sugar until the mixture forms a paste and is smooth and crack free. Keep airtight and store in a refrigerator. Bring back to room temperature before use.

Amount of CMC can be varied depending on humidity and your preference for stiffness of paste.

QUICK FLOWER PASTE RECIPE

As above, but add 2–3 generous tsp white vegetable fat. Add a drop of vanilla essence, lemon extract or rose water for aroma.

SUGAR STICKS

These are used as edible supports, mainly to help hold modelled heads in place.

Makes around 10-12 sticks

- 5 ml (1 level tsp) stiff peak royal icing
- 1.25 ml (¼ tsp) CMC or gum tragacanth
- Icing (powdered) sugar in a sugar shaker

Knead the gum into the royal icing until the mixture thickens and forms a paste, adding a small amount of icing (powdered) sugar if the mixture is a little wet. Either roll out and cut into different sized strips of various lengths using a plain-bladed knife, or roll individual thin sausages of paste. Leave to dry overnight on a sheet of foam. When dry, store in an airtight container.

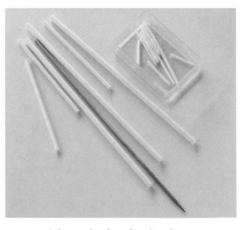

Sugar sticks and other food-safe supports

Basic techniques

Cake decorating is easier than it looks, although it can seem a little daunting if you are a complete beginner. This section shows you a few simple, basic techniques that will help you achieve great results and professional-looking cakes.

Keep the knife flat to cake surface to remove crust

Roll out evenly using a sprinkling of icing (powdered) sugar

SCULPTING A CAKE

The first rule of cake sculpting is to have a moist but firm sponge cake that will not crumble. I recommend that you follow the recipes and method given in this book for a Butter sponge cake (see page 7). If you are tempted to buy a cake mix or a ready-baked cake, make sure that it won't crumble away as soon as you start to cut into it. Ready-made cakes are really only suitable for projects involving minimal sculpting and stacking of layers.

Use a serrated knife for cake carving. When trimming away the crust of a cake, keep the cake level so there are no problems with balance if the cake is being stacked. Use a ruler for straight cuts and be aware of the knife blade, keeping it in the correct position for the cut you need.

ROLLING OUT SUGARPASTE

Sugarpaste can be rolled out successfully on any even food-safe work surface, but I recommend that you use a large polypropylene board and rolling pin, both of which have tough, smooth surfaces.

Start by kneading the sugarpaste, until soft and warm. Sugarpaste can start to dry out when exposed to the air, so roll out as quickly and evenly as possible to a covering thickness of around 3–4mm ($\frac{1}{8}$ in), moving the paste around after each roll using a sprinkling of icing (powdered) sugar. Make sure there isn't a build up of sugarpaste or icing (powdered) sugar on either your board or your rolling pin, to help keep the sugarpaste perfectly smooth. Sugarpaste can stick to the work surface very quickly. If this happens, re-knead and start again.

COLOURING SUGARPASTE

Some brands of ready-made sugarpaste are available in a range of colours but I usually prefer to mix my own colours. The best food colourings are obtainable as a paste or concentrated liquid. Avoid the watery liquid food colourings and powder colours, unless you want to achieve very pale shades. Powder food colours are usually only used to enhance certain areas.

Sugarpaste blocks

Knead paste until colour is even

Lift the sugarpaste using a rolling pin

Roll the sugarpaste gently over the cake

Any excess icing (powdered) sugar can be brushed off using dried sugarpaste. With stubborn areas, use a slightly damp large soft bristle pastry brush. The moisture will melt the excess, but take care not to wet the surface as streaks may result.

The best way to apply food colour paste is with the tip of a knife. Simply dab a block of sugarpaste with the end of a knife (if you are creating a new colour, remember to keep a record of how many 'dabs' of paste you use). Add a little at a time until the required shade is achieved. Knead thoroughly after each addition until the colour is even. Bear in mind that the colour will deepen slightly on standing, so be careful not to add too much.

If you wish to colour a large amount of sugarpaste, colour a small ball first, and then knead into the remaining amount to disperse the colour quickly. Wearing plastic gloves or rubbing a little white vegetable fat over your hands can help when colouring with deep shades, as this can prevent a lot of mess. Some food colours can temporarily stain your hands.

COVERING A CAKE BOARD WITH SUGARPASTE

Knead the sugarpaste thoroughly until soft and warm. Roll out to roughly the size and shape of the cake board, using a sprinkling of icing (powdered) sugar and move around after each roll to prevent sticking. Roll to a thickness of 2-3mm.

Place the rolling pin on the centre of the rolled out sugarpaste and lift the back half over the top. Hold both ends of the rolling pin, lift and position the sugarpaste against the cake board and unroll over the top. Roll the rolling pin gently over the surface to stick the sugarpaste firmly to the board. If the sugarpaste is still loose, moisten along the outside edge only, using a little water or edible glue on a brush.

Rub the surface with a cake smoother for a smooth, dimple-free surface. Lift the cake board and trim away the excess around the outside edge using a plain-bladed knife. Keep the knife straight to gain a neat edge, carefully removing any residue along the blade for a clean cut.

COVERING A CAKE WITH SUGARPASTE

Before applying sugarpaste to the buttercream-covered surface of a cake, make sure the buttercream is soft and sticky by reworking a little using a knife, or by adding a little more. Roll the sugarpaste out approximately 15cm (6in) larger than the top of the cake to allow enough icing to cover the sides of the cake. You can lift and position the sugarpaste

on the cake as you would to cover a cake board, and then press the sugarpaste gently but firmly in position, smoothing over the surface using your hands. Rub gently with your hands over any small cracks to blend them in. If you have any gaps, stroke the sugarpaste surface to stretch it slightly. Trim away any excess using a plain-bladed knife.

OBTAINING A GOOD FINISH

You will invariably find that you have occasional bumps on the surface of your cake or trapped air bubbles. A cake smoother is invaluable for obtaining a perfectly smooth finish for your sugarpaste. Rub firmly but gently in a circular motion.

CAKE LAYER CUTTER

It can be quite tricky for a non-professional cake decorator to cut even layers in cakes. Someone with experience usually uses a large serrated knife. Some use wooden or plastic strips to the height they need for the layer placed on opposite sides of the cake and use these as cutting guides either using a knife or stretching a food-safe wire or strong thread against them and gently pulling through using a sawing action. For ease, I recommend a cake layer cutter or leveller. These are food-safe, height adjustable wires on frames with a raised handle on top that gently slices through your cake. To use, simply place the layer cutter against the cake and gently push backwards and forwards using a sawing action slicing through the cake.

Dust away excess icing (powdered) sugar using a large brush

General equipment

There is a huge selection of cake decorating tools and equipment available now. Listed below are the basic necessities for cake decorating, some of which you are likely to already have in your kitchen. I've also added some specialist items that can help achieve great results.

Bakeware

The basic round and square tins in different sizes are an essential for cake decorators. I recommend purchasing the good quality tins and they should last a lifetime.

There is a plethora of choice for bakeware with silicone now avaliable as it comes not only in rounds and squares but in a variety of different shapes. The basic small bowl shape can be obtained in silicone as seperate bowls or in sheet form. You can, of course, bake in ovenproof glass and Pyrex ovenproof bowls are available from most supermarkets and kitchenware stores in a variety of different sizes. There are now also spherical or dome/bowl-shaped tins available, which you can use to bake your cake. For both the tins and ovenproof bowls, you just need to grease well and pop a small circle of greaseproof paper at the bottom to prepare for baking.

Workboard

You can easily work on any washable, even work surface, but for best results use a non-stick polypropylene work board. They are available in various sizes, with non-slip feet on the reverse.

Rolling pins

Polypropylene rolling pins are available in a variety of lengths, but basic large and small pins are the most useful.

Serrated knife

A medium-sized serrated knife is invaluable when sculpting a cake, as it cuts away neatly when using a slight sawing action.

Plain-bladed knife

Small and medium plain-bladed knives are used to cut through paste cleanly and evenly. Choose knives with ultra-fine blades for neat, clean cuts and make sure the handle and blade are well balanced.

Palette knife

This is used for the smooth spreading of buttercream, and also to help lift modelled pieces easily from a work surface.

Cake smoother

Smoothes the surface of sugarpaste to remove any bumps or indents by rubbing gently in a circular motion.

Sugar shaker

A handy container filled with icing (powdered) sugar. Used for sprinkling the work surface before rolling out paste.

Paintbrushes

Available in various sizes, choose good quality sable paintbrushes for painting details. Use a flat-ended brush for dusting powder food colours over the surface of dried paste.

Large pastry brush

Invaluable for brushing excess icing (powdered) sugar and crumbs away. When dampened slightly, it will lift any stubborn residue icing (powdered) sugar from the surface quickly and easily.

Ruler

Used for approximate measuring during cake and paste cutting and for indenting neat lines in sugarpaste.

Scissors

Needed for general use of cutting templates, piping bags and some small detailing.

Plain piping tubes

Not only are these tubes used for piping royal icing, they are also used as cutters and indenters. For finer cuts use good quality metal tubes in preference to plastic ones.

Paper piping bags

For use with royal icing. Parchment or greaseproof paper piping bags are available ready-made from cake decorating suppliers.

Cocktail sticks

Readily available in food-safe wood or plastic form, these are useful for marking any fine detailing in paste.

Foam pieces

Used to support modelled pieces whilst drying, as the air can circulate all around. When the piece is dry, the foam is easily removable.

Internal supports/dowels

I use large plastic dowelling if I need something extra to help hold items upright and in place on the cake, i.e. , castle towers or toadstool stems . For internal supports in our figures, preferably use sugar sticks so they are completely edible and safe (see page 16 for recipe) or as a substitute use small paper lolly sticks. Don't be tempted to use cocktail sticks (toothpicks) as these are sharp and could cause injury.

Cutters

Available in an array of different styles and shapes. Metal cutters usually have finer, cleaner edges but are more expensive. Some small cutters have plungers to remove the cut out shape.

Turntable

When working on a cake, placing on a turntable allows you to quickly and easily move the cake around. Some bakers find it invaluable as it lifts the cake to a higher level.

Food colouring

Paste colours are suitable for colouring paste and royal icing, while powder colours add a subtle hue when brushed onto the surface of dried sugarpaste.

Dotty dog

What you will need

See pages 7 to 19 for recipes and techniques.

- 1 x 15 cm (6 in) and 1 x 20 cm (8 in) dia. bowl-shaped cakes
- 450 g (1 lb/2 c) cake filling
- Icing (powdered) sugar in a sugar shaker

Sugarpaste

- 770 g (1 lb 11 oz) blue
- 1.25 kg (2 lb 12 oz) pale blue
- 35 g (1¼ oz) dark blue
- Small ball of black

- Edible glue

Equipment

- 30 cm (14 in) round cake board
- Large rolling pin
- Small plain bladed knife
- Serrated carving knife
- Palette knife
- Cake smoother
- No.2 sable paintbrush (for edible glue)

This cute dog is not only gorgeous with his innocent expression but also a beautifully simple design, appropriate for so many occasions.

1 Using 450 g (1 lb) of blue sugarpaste, roll out and cover the cake board (see page 18, how to cover a cake board) and then set aside to dry.

2 Trim the crust from each cake, level the tops keeping the edges slightly rounded and then turn over and cut a central layer in each. Sandwich the layers together and position on the cake board with a little space in between each. Spread a layer over the surface as a crumb coat to seal the cake and help the sugarpaste stick.

tip

Leave the buttercreamed cake surface to set before covering. This will help prevent layers slipping.

Covering the cake board

Positioning the cakes on the cake board

Smoothing the sugarpaste

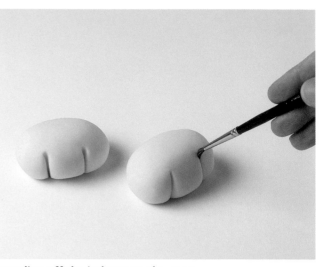

Rounding off the indents on the paws

3 Using 900 g (2 lb) of pale blue sugarpaste, roll out and cover the two cakes together, smoothing down and around the shape. Trim excess from around the edge and then smooth underneath. To gain a smooth surface, roll some trimmings into a small ball and rub in a circular motion over the sugarpaste covered surface until completely smooth and dimple free. This will also remove any excess icing (powdered) sugar and produce a clean finish.

4 For his tail, roll 35 g (1¼ oz) of pale blue into a teardrop shape, press down on the full end and stick in position curled round slightly. Put aside 5 g (¼ oz) of pale blue for later and then split the remainder into four equal pieces for his paws. Roll each into oval shapes and then indent twice using the back of a knife. Use the tip of a paintbrush to round off each indent at the top and then stick each paw in position turned outwards.

5 To make ears, split 175 g (6 oz) of blue sugarpaste in half, roll into teardrop shapes and press flat with the cake smoother. For his muzzle, roll 115 g (4 oz) of blue sugarpaste into an oval shape and stick in position on his face and resting on the cake board.

6 Shape the remaining blue sugarpaste into different sized flattened pieces for patches, adding one onto his eye area. Roll two small black oval-shaped eyes.

7 Using the dark blue, roll out and cut a strip for his collar and add tiny circles of pale blue over the surface. Roll the remaining dark blue into a rounded teardrop shape and stick in position for his nose, holding for a few moments until secure.

Rear view of the finished cake

Swamp monster

What you will need

See pages 7 to 19 for recipes and techniques.

- 23 cm (9 in) bowl-shaped cake or dome-shaped tin (pan)
- 450 g (1 lb/2 c) cake filling
- Icing (powdered) sugar in a sugar shaker

Sugarpaste
- 565 g (1 lb 4 oz) lime green
- 1.1 kg (2 lb 6¾ oz) green
- 45 g (1½ oz) black
- 100 g (3½ oz) white

Modelling paste
- 20 g (¾ oz) white
- 30 g (1 oz) blue
- 15 g (½ oz) skin-tone
- 5 g (¼ oz) pale yellow
- Tiny piece of black

- Edible glue
- Lime green piping gel
- Pink powder colour

Equipment
- 35 cm (14 in) petal-shaped cake board
- 23 cm (9 in) round cake card
- Large rolling pin
- Small plain bladed knife
- Serrated carving knife
- Palette knife
- Cake smoother
- No.2 sable paintbrush (for edible glue)
- Dusting brush

Here's a quick and simple three-eyed swamp monster oozing with lots of gunky green slime. The little boy is optional of course, depending on whether they've been good or not!

Covering the cake with sugarpaste

Smooth a line for the top lip

Cake board

1 Using 450 g (1 lb) of lime green sugarpaste, roll out and cover the cake board (see page 18, how to cover a cake board). Smooth ripples around the shape of the cake board using your fingertip and then set aside to dry.

Cake

2 Trim the crust from the cake and level the top. Cut two layers in the cake. Check the cake card is the same circumference as the cake and trim if necessary. Using a little filling, assemble the cake onto the cake card and sandwich all layers together. Spread a layer over the surface of the cake as a crumb coat to seal the cake and help the sugarpaste stick.

3 Roll out 800 g (1 lb 12 oz) of green sugarpaste and cover the cake completely, smoothing down and around the shape and then trim excess from around the base. Position the cake on the cake board. Roll a small ball of trimmings and rub over the sugarpaste surface to smooth out any dimples.

4 Cut out the mouth area measuring 15 cm (6 in) width, removing the sugarpaste covering and then thinly roll out black sugarpaste and fill the space, smoothing around the shape. Smooth the top lip with your fingertip to further indent the mouth outline.

5 Split 225 g (8 oz) of green sugarpaste into four pieces. For tentacles, roll long thin tapering sausage shapes and stick in position using a little edible glue. Curl one around ready for the boy.

6 Split 35 g (1¼ oz) of white sugarpaste in half and roll the two smaller eyes. Roll the large eye using 45 g (1½ oz) and stick all in position with an eyelid covering the top of each using the remaining green sugarpaste. Model flattened circles of white sugarpaste for teeth. Add oval shaped black pupils using the black sugarpaste trimmings.

7 For scales, model different sized flattened circles of lime green sugarpaste, indenting into the centre of each with your fingertip. Stick these over the cake surface. Roll different sized balls and stick in place around the cake.

Boy

7 To make the trousers, roll the blue modelling paste into a sausage shape and press down to flatten slightly. Make a cut three quarters the length to separate legs and then smooth the cut to soften, pinching gently half way to shape the knees. Stick in position against the tentacle and resting on the cake board.

8 Model two white oval shaped shoes and stick in position turned slightly outwards. Using the remaining white for his top, roll into an oval shape, press down to flatten slightly and then cut either side to separate sleeves. Smooth along the cut edges to soften and bend each half way to shape elbows. Make a small hole in the bottom of each sleeve ready for hands and then stick the top in position against the cake.

9 For the boy's head, roll 10 g (¼ oz) of skin-tone modelling paste into an oval shape, flatten the facial area slightly and then push the end of a paintbrush into the bottom to open the wide mouth. Add a tiny oval shaped nose and two oval shaped ears, each indented slightly using the end of a paintbrush. Model two tiny oval-shaped black eyes and fill his mouth with a tiny flattened ball. Brush a little pink powder colour over his cheeks.

Modelling the boy's head

10 Moisten the end of each sleeve with edible glue and wait to become tacky. Meanwhile, split the remaining skin-tone modelling paste in half and use for hands. Model teardrop shapes and press down to flatten slightly. Make a cut on one side for the thumb and three further cuts along the top, ensuring they are straight and roll each gently to stretch and round off. Push the thumb down towards the palm. Roll the opposite end to gain excess to push up into each sleeve, sticking the hands securely.

Spooning the piping gel around the cake

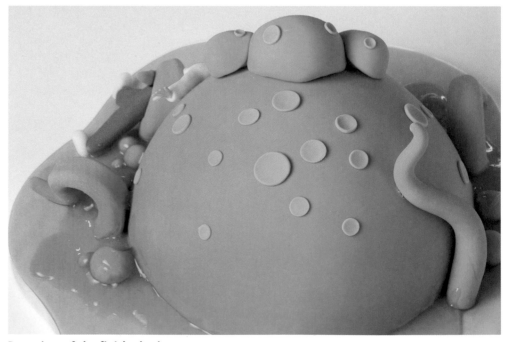

Rear view of the finished cake

Cloud castle

What you will need

See pages 7 to 19 for recipes and techniques.

- 28 x 7–8 cm (2½–3 in) dome-shaped cakes or 14 x cupcakes
- 315 g (11 oz/1½ c) cake filling
- Icing (powdered) sugar in a sugar shaker

Sugarpaste
- 400 g (14 oz) pale lilac
- 800 g (1 lb 12 oz) white

Modelling paste
- 340 g (12 oz) white
- 60 g (2 oz) lilac
- 15 g (½ oz) pink
- 15 g (½ oz) pale pink
- 10 g (¼ oz) blue
- Tiny piece of black

- Edible glue
- Blue, pink and purple powder food colouring
- Edible or food-safe white glitter

Equipment
- 30 cm (12 in) round cake board
- Large rolling pin
- Small plain bladed knife
- Serrated carving knife
- Palette knife
- Cake smoother
- A few cocktail sticks
- No.2 sable paintbrush (for edible glue)
- Length of food-safe dowelling
- No.1 & no.3 (PME) piping tube (tip)
- Miniature star cutter

Every little girl dreams of a castle in the sky. Here is one of the prettiest, floating on a big fluffy cloud, complete with two gorgeous sparkling fairies.

Spread cake filling over the cake surface as a crumb coat

1 Using a sprinkling of icing (powdered) sugar to prevent sticking, roll out the lilac sugarpaste to a thickness of 2–3 mm (¹⁄₈ in), lift carefully using the rolling pin and use to cover the cake board. Smooth the surface with a cake smoother by rubbing gently in a circular motion and then trim excess from around the edge. Put aside to dry.

2 Sandwich all the cakes together with cake filling, making fourteen spherical shapes. If using cupcakes, remove the paper case and trim around the top edge to round off slightly. Arrange eleven cakes on the cake board with three grouped together centrally on top. Spread a layer of filling over the surface of the cakes as a crumb coat and to help the sugarpaste stick.

3 Roll out the white sugarpaste and cover the cakes completely, smoothing down and around the shape, stretching out pleats and tucking in around the base. Trim away excess and use the knife to push the covering underneath. Roll a 30 g (1 oz) ball of white trimmings and use as a cake smoother, rubbing over the surface in a circular motion.

4 Roll a sausage for the large central tower using 45 g (1½ oz) of white modelling paste. Roll to a length of 12 cm (5 in) and then gently push the dowel down through the centre, leaving some protruding at the bottom. This will be inserted into the centre of the cake and hold the tower steady. Indent a window near the top by pressing in with the end of a paintbrush and gently moving up and down to open up. Mark a swirl pattern over the surface of the tower by pressing in with the tip of a cocktail stick. Set the tower aside to dry on a flat surface.

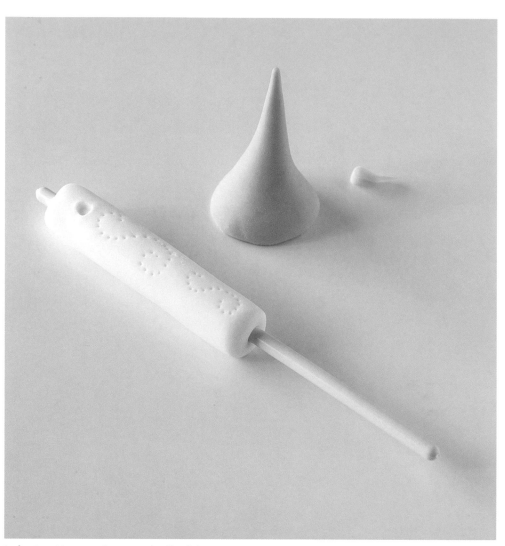

Indent patterns using a cocktail stick

Cut the slanted roof by slicing down at an angle

5 Make four more different sized towers, two using 30 g (1 oz) of white modelling paste for each and 15 g (½ oz) each for the smaller two. Roll in the centre of the two larger to narrow slightly and mark windows and pattern as before. Stick the tall tower in position with the smaller towers arranged around it.

6 For the house shape, knead 75 g (2½ oz) of modelling paste into a ball and press down with a cake smoother to flatten, putting more pressure on one side to narrow. Repeat for the opposite side. Cut either side to straighten. To shape the roof, slice away at the top cutting downwards, turn over and repeat on the opposite side making the pointed roof.

7 Indent a window at the front and then stick in position resting against the tall tower. Thinly roll out 20 g (¾ oz) and cut an oblong for the roof and then mark the spiral pattern as before.

8 Make the two thin towers, the large archway and the arched tower at the front of the pathway using white modelling paste. To make the large archway, roll a 30 g (1 oz) ball and press down to flatten slightly. Cut the bottom straight and then cut out the arch using a knife, smoothing it gently by rolling with the paintbrush handle. Cut either side to straighten, cutting more away on the right hand side so the arch is higher and sits neatly against the tower. Make the small arched tower cutting the opening as before and then pinch around the top to round off and narrow slightly.

9 Roll 20 g (¾ oz) of white modelling paste into a long thin sausage and cut a strip for the pathway. Stick in position curling between the arched tower and large archway.

10 Make the large central tower roof first using 35 g (1¼ oz) of lilac modelling paste. Roll into a teardrop shape and roll the narrow end into a sharp point. Press down on the full end to flatten and then pinch and smooth gently around the outside edge to widen. Stick in position with a little edible glue. Make the remaining tower roofs using the lilac, pink and pale pink modelling paste.

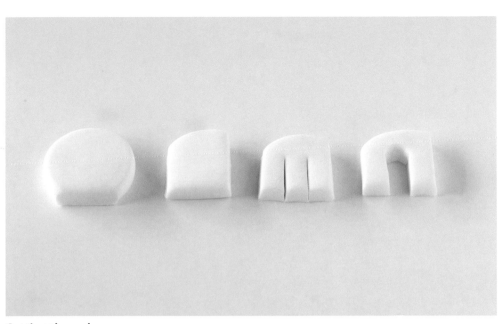

Cutting the archway

11 Using pea-sized amounts of white, roll out and cut long triangles for the flags, wrapping one each around the top of the three tallest tower roofs and securing with edible glue.

12 To make the clouds, roll 20 g (¾ oz) of white into three slightly different sized oval shapes, press down to flatten slightly and then press in around the outside edge of each using the back of a knife. Stick the clouds in position holding for a few moments until secure.

Fairies

13 Make their wands first by rolling two minute sausages of blue modelling paste, add a tiny star to the top then set aside to dry. To make their dresses, split the remaining blue in half and roll into teardrop shapes. Press down to flatten each slightly and mark pleats using the paintbrush handle. Using pea-sized amounts of skin-tone for each make the four legs by rolling into tiny sausages

rounding off each end. Bend each end round and squeeze to narrow and lengthen the foot. Stick each leg onto the back of the dress and then stick the dresses in position on the cake.

14 For arms, split two pea-sized amounts of skin-tone each in half and roll into tiny sausages, pinching each gently at one end to round off the hand. Stick in place with a fairy wand. Note: Take care with the wand handles as they are so fine they will be fragile.

15 Split the remaining skin-tone in half and make their ball-shaped heads with minute oval-shaped noses. Mark smiles with the tip of the no.3 piping tube pushed in at an upwards angle and dimple the corners using a cocktail stick. Indent small holes for eye sockets using the end of a paintbrush and then stick each head in position. To make their eyes, roll out the black modelling paste and cut four tiny circles using the no.1 piping tube.

16 To make their hair, moisten around the head area of each with a little edible glue and then roll tiny different sized balls of white modelling paste building up little by little until the head is covered.

To finish

17 Dust around the cake board and castle with the powder colours, adding the colour little by little until intense in places and then sprinkle the edible or food-safe glitter around the cake.

Alien spaceship

What you will need

See pages 7 to 19 for recipes and techniques.

- 1 x 20 cm (8 in) and 1 x 15 cm (6 in) dia. bowl shaped cakes
- 450 g (1 lb/2 c) cake filling
- Icing (powdered) sugar in a sugar shaker

Sugarpaste
- 700 g (1 lb 8¾ oz) purple
- 820 g (1 lb 13 oz) red

Modelling paste
- 20 g (¾ oz) purple
- 85 g (2¾ oz) lime green
- 15 g (½ oz) white
- 60 g (2 oz) black
- 60 g (2 oz) red

- Edible glue
- Edible silver colouring
- 6 sugar sticks or food-safe internal supports
- Dark blue powder food colouring

Equipment
- 30 cm (12 in) round cake board
- 20 cm (8 in) round cake card
- Cake smoother
- 1 cm (½ in), 2.5 cm (1 in) and 6 cm (2½ in) circle cutters
- 3 lengths of food-safe plastic dowelling
- Large rolling pin
- Small plain bladed knife
- Serrated carving knife
- Palette knife
- Food-safe cotton thread
- No.2 sable paintbrush (for edible glue)
- No.1, 2, 3 & 4 (PME) piping tubes (tips)
- Dusting brush
- Template (see page 124)

With his infectiously silly grin and cute expression this alien certainly looks happy to be visiting from outer space.

Place the cut-out circle into the bowl to shape the door

1 Using a sprinkling of icing (powdered) sugar to prevent sticking, roll out 400 g (14 oz) of purple sugarpaste to a thickness of 2–3 mm and use to cover the cake board. Rub the surface with a cake smoother, pressing firmly but gently and move over the surface in a circular motion to remove dimples and then set aside to dry.

2 To allow for drying time make the small round door for the top of the spaceship first. Roll out the purple modelling paste and cut a 6 cm (2½ in) circle. Dust the small bowl with icing (powdered) sugar and place the circle of paste into it smoothing around the shape. Leave to set in the bowl for an hour or so checking now and then to ensure that it hasn't stuck and then remove. Using a little edible glue, push a sugar stick or food-

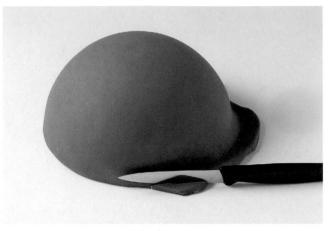

Trim excess from around the base

safe internal support into the side until held secure (this will help hold the door in position later). Set aside to dry completely.

3 Trim the crust from each cake and level the tops. Cut two layers in each and then sandwich back together with cake filling. Spread a layer over the dome-shaped surface of both cakes as a crumb coat and to help the sugarpaste stick.

4 Roll out 450 g (1 lb) of red sugarpaste and cover the larger cake completely, smoothing down and around the shape and trimming excess from around the edge. To smooth the surface, take a small ball of red sugarpaste and rub over the covering; this is perfect for smoothing out any dimples and surface imperfections. Turn over and spread the top with cake filling.

5 To support the top part of the spaceship, push three dowels down into the centre of the large cake, not exceeding 8 cm (3 in) in diameter. Mark each at the top and remove. Place the dowels down on the work surface and cut to the same height following the shortest mark and then insert back into the cake until they are level with the top surface. Position the cake centrally on the cake board.

6 Roll out the remaining red sugarpaste and use to cover the cake card and then position this on top of the large bowl-shaped cake. Cover the join around the outside edge with a 2 cm (¾ in) wide strip of red modelling paste. To measure the circumference use a length of food-safe thread and cut to size.

7 Cover the small cake using the remaining purple sugarpaste smoothing the surface as before. Spread a layer of cake filling on the red covered board and then position this cake onto it.

8 Cut out the oblong window in the centre and two circular windows either side using the 2.5 cm (1 in) circle cutter. Cut out the doorway at the top using the larger circle cutter. Cut out small windows spaced evenly around the bottom using the 1 cm (½ in) circle cutter. Thinly roll out black and cut pieces to fill the spaces.

9 Cut out red and green circles for the lights using the smallest cutter and stick edging around the cake. Roll four thin sausages for the stabilizers and insert a small sugar stick down through them leaving a little protruding at each end and stick in place evenly spaced at the bottom of the spaceship. Cut out four red circles for the landing pads using the 2.5 cm (1 in) circle cutter and push into the centre of each to cup them gently and stick into position.

10 To make the alien, first make a flattened circle of green for the bottom of his neck using 5 g (just under ¼ oz) of lime green modelling paste and smooth inside to widen and create a ridge around the outside edge.

11 For his head, roll 60 g (2 oz) of lime green into a ball and then pinch and roll to make his neck. Squeeze to widen his head making it more oval-shaped. Indent his mouth by pressing in with the template (see page 124) and then remove. Stroke smile lines around the outside corners of the mouth area using the paintbrush handle.

Push dowels down into the cake until level with the top

12 Using the mouth template, thinly roll out black modelling paste and cut out the shape to fill the mouth. Stick into position and then add tiny white teeth. Push a sugar stick or internal support down into the neck and then push the head down over it securing at the bottom with a little edible glue. Indent two holes either side of his head ready for his ears later using a cocktail stick.

13 Roll 5 g (just under ¼ oz) of lime green into a ball and roll out a sausage from one end rounding it off slightly making the nose. Place down on the work surface and press down on the eye area to flatten slightly. Pinch the top of the nose and then indent nostrils with the end of a paintbrush.

Build up the shapes to create the alien's head

14 Roll a white oval-shape for the eye and press down to flatten. Stick onto the eye area with a small black pupil. Stick the eye and nose in position onto the alien's face with a piece of rolled up kitchen paper supporting the back until dry.

15 Roll two tiny sausages for the ears along with two small pea-sized circles indented in the centre.

16 Split the remaining lime green modelling paste in half and use to make the hands. To make a hand, roll one into a ball and pinch and roll out a sausage shaped arm. Press down on the rounded end to flatten and then make a cut on one side for the thumb cutting down half way between the top and the wrist.

17 Make two more slightly shorter cuts along the top to separate fingers. Pinch the thumb and fingers to round off and indent knuckles. Make the second hand and then push gently into each palm so the hand curves slightly.

18 Roll the remaining red into a long teardrop shape for the tongue and mark down the centre from the narrow end using a knife. Curl the tongue around and stick in position holding for a few moments until secure, or use a small piece of rolled up kitchen paper to hold in place until dry.

19 Stick the door in position by moistening the area with a little edible glue and then gently pushing the door with the sugar stick inside down into the covering. Use a little rolled up kitchen paper to support until dry.

20 Dust the dark blue powder colouring over the surface of the cake board and then paint swirls and spirals using the silver colouring.

Using the paste trimmings, make the different sized planets by pressing down a ball. Cut lots of tiny white circles using the piping tubes.

Back view

Ted in a box

What you will need

See pages 7 to 19 for recipes and techniques.

- 2 x 15 cm (6 in) square cakes, 6 cm (2½ in) depth
- 2 x 11 cm (4½ in) bowl-shaped cakes, 5 cm (2 in) depth
- 450 g (1 lb/2 c) cake filling
- Icing (powdered) sugar in a sugar shaker

Sugarpaste
- 650 g (1 lb 7 oz) pale green
- 1.7 kg (3 lb 12 oz) pale pink

Pastillage
- 375 g (12 oz) cream

Modelling paste
- 260 g (9 oz) pale green
- 145 g (5 oz) cream
- 5 g (¼ oz) black

Royal icing
- 30 g (1 oz) cream

- Edible glue
- Edible silver colouring
- Sugar stick or food-safe internal support
- Pink powder food colouring

Equipment
- 30 cm (12 in) square cake board
- 1 x 15 cm (6 in) square cake card
- 1 x 10 cm (4 in) round cake card
- Cake smoother
- 3 x food-safe plastic dowelling
- Large and small rolling pins
- Small plain bladed knife
- Serrated carving knife
- Palette knife
- Ruler
- No.2 sable paintbrush (for edible glue)
- 2 cm (¾ in) and 3 cm (1¼ in) circle cutters
- Paper piping bag
- Dusting brush

Here's a gorgeous teddy bear present style cake in extremely pretty and appealing ice-cream colours, perfect for any young girl's special celebration.

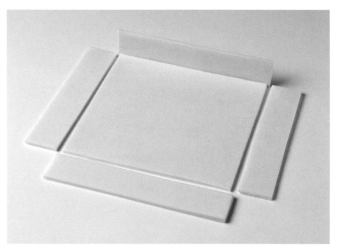

Check the box lid sides are cut correctly then leave to dry

Cake board

1 Using 450 g (1 lb) of pale green sugarpaste, roll out and cover the cake board (see page 18, how to cover a cake board) and then set aside to dry.

Box lid

2 Thinly roll out the Pastillage and cut an 18 cm (7 in) square. Cut four strips for the sides, two 18 cm (7 in) in length and two 0.5 cm (¼ in) longer to allow for the overlap at the join. Set everything aside to dry completely. As the pieces dry, move them slightly to ensure they are not sticking to the surface and when the top surface has dried, flip over to dry the reverse.

3 Thinly roll out pink and green modelling paste and cut different sized circles to decorate the box lid, sticking each in position as they are made.

4 When the box lid pieces are dry, assemble using royal icing to stick the side pieces in position. If there is any excess royal icing, wipe away gently with your fingers. Set aside to dry completely.

Box cake

5 Trim the crust from each square cake, level the tops and then cut a layer in each. Check the cake card is the same size as the cake and trim if necessary. Using a little filling, assemble the cake onto the cake card and sandwich all layers together. Spread a layer over the surface of the cake as a crumb coat to seal the cake and help the sugarpaste stick. Trim the crust from each bowl shaped cake and sandwich together and crumb coat as before.

6 Roll out the remaining pale green sugarpaste to a thickness of 3–4mm and use to cover the top of the cake, ensuring the sides are cut perfectly. Smooth with a cake smoother and use to push back any distortion around the edge.

7 Using 900 g (2 lb) of pale pink sugarpaste roll out and cut pieces to cover the sides of the cake, 2 cm (¾ in) higher than the top. Cover the sides first then the back and front. Secure the joins closed with edible glue.

> **tip**
>
> If your sugarpaste cut sides are soft, leave to firm slightly before positioning against the cake sides.

Use a cake smoother to smooth the covering

8 Push the three dowels down through the box cake centrally, keeping them within 10 cm (4 in) diameter within the cake card circumference being used for the teddy. Mark the top of each, remove and score to the lowest measurement if there is a difference. To break the dowelling, hold either side of the score, bend and snap to break. Gently push the dowelling back into the cake until level with the surface.

Secure the dry lid against the cake with a little royal icing

Teddy

9 Prepare the dome shaped cakes as before, sandwiching them together making a spherical. Roll out 400 g (14 oz) of pale pink sugarpaste and cover the cake completely, smoothing and stretching out pleats and trimming excess from around the base. Use a golf-sized ball of sugarpaste to rub over the surface as a cake smoother to remove any surface imperfections. Mark a central line using the back of a knife and then rub along the line with your fingertip to soften.

10 Roll out 115 g (4 oz) of pale pink and use to cover the cake card. Smooth around the outside edge to make the covering dome-shaped. Mark a central line as before and then press a small dip in the centre. Stick the head onto the centre and then position onto the top of the box cake using a little edible glue to secure.

11 Thinly roll out cream and pale green modelling paste a little at a time and cut different sized strips to decorate the box using a ruler to ensure straight lines.

tip

Leave the cut strips to firm up slightly before positioning to help keep any distortion to a minimum.

The shapes to build up Teddy's face

12 For his muzzle, roll 60 g (2 oz) of pale pink into a fat teardrop shape and press down to flatten slightly. Mark a line down the centre as before. For ears, split 45 g (1½ oz) of pale pink and roll into ball shapes, indenting into the centre with the end of the small rolling pin. Using 10 g (¼ oz) of pale pink roll his teardrop shaped nose. To give him a blush, brush a little edible pink powder colour over his nose and cheeks. Roll two oval-shaped eyes with black, modelling paste.

13 Split the remaining pink sugarpaste in half and model his two arms, both tapering down slightly at each paw. Stick these in position resting against the box sides, holding for a few moments to secure.

14 To make Ted's bow, split 90 g (3 oz) of pale green modelling paste in half and roll into sausage shapes both tapering at each end. Press flat with a cake smoother. Smooth around the outside of each shape to flatten further and then loop over and secure closed with a little edible glue. Stick in position with a small flattened circle for the bow centre.

15 For the bow ties, roll out the remaining pale green and cut two strips both tapering narrower at the top. Cut a 'v' shape from the bottom of each and then mark pleats with the paintbrush handle.

16 To finish, stick the dried box lid in position resting against the box securing with a little royal icing underneath.

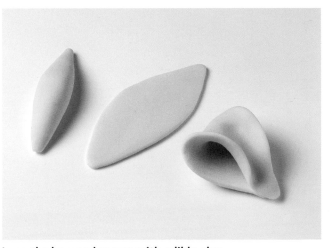

Loop the bow and secure with edible glue

37

Pirate skull

What you will need

See pages 7 to 19 for recipes and techniques.

- 2 x 15 cm (6 in) round cakes
- 1 x 15 cm (6 in) bowl-shaped cake
- 625 g (1 lb 6 oz/2¾ c) cake filling
- Icing (powdered) sugar in a sugar shaker

Sugarpaste
- 450 g (1 lb) dark grey
- 315 g (11 oz) black
- 315 g (11 oz) cream
- 370 g (13 oz) red

Modelling paste
- 20 g (¾ oz) black
- Small piece of brown
- 145 g (5 oz) white
- 10 g (¼ oz) red
- 10 g (¼ oz) blue

- Edible glue
- Red and Brown food colouring
- 1 tbsp cooled, boiled water
- Edible or food-safe gold and silver food colouring

Equipment
- 30 cm (12 in) round cake board
- Large rolling pin
- Small plain bladed knife
- Serrated carving knife
- Palette knife
- No.4 (PME) piping tube (tip)
- 4 cm (1½ in), 3cm (1¼ in) & 2.5 cm (1 in) circle cutters
- A few cocktail sticks
- No.2 sable paintbrush (for edible glue)
- No.6 sable paintbrush

The intrigue of hidden treasure is always appealing. It's found here with a gruesome skull guarding its secret of gold, silver and jewels.

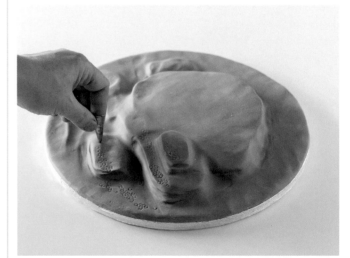

Mark the texture using the piping tube (tip)

1 Trim the crust from each cake and level the tops. Cut a layer centrally in each cake. Set aside all the cakes except for one of the 15 cm (6 in) round layers. From this, cut another layer placing one centrally on the cake board securing with a little cake filling.

2 Cut angular shapes from the second piece and sandwich these pieces onto the cake board building up the stepped rock effect and then spread a layer over the surface of the cake as a crumb coat and to help the sugarpaste stick.

3 Using a sprinkling of icing (powdered) sugar to prevent sticking, roll out the dark grey sugarpaste to a thickness of 3-4mm (⅛ in)and use to cover the cake and board completely. Smooth around the shapes and pinch edges for a rock effect. Indent the sides by pressing in with the paintbrush handle. Mark the texture on the surface using the piping tube (tip).

4 For the skull, stack the remaining cakes together with the bowl-shaped cake on top. The height of the skull at this stage should be around 15 cm (6 in). Trim around the sides so the cake slopes down narrower around the base. Sandwich all layers together and crumb coat as before and position on the cake board with a little cake filling underneath to secure.

5 Thinly roll out the black sugarpaste and cut a strip the height of the cake and 35 cm (14 in) in length. Dust with icing (powdered) sugar and then roll up both ends until they meet in the centre. Lift this rolled up piece of sugarpaste and place against the front of the cake. Unroll around it, trim away excess and rub the join closed at the back using a little edible glue.

6 Roll 45 g (1½ oz) of cream sugarpaste into a sausage rounding off either end slightly and use to pad out the chin area. Split 25 g (just over ¾ oz) and use to shape the two cheekbones and then roll a thin sausage for the nose and stick in the centre of his face shaping an upside down heart shape.

7 Thickly roll out the remaining cream sugarpaste and cover the skull's face completely, smoothing around the contours of the shapes underneath. Cut around the shape as shown in the step picture. Cut out his mouth, nose and eyes, revealing the black covering underneath. Cut cracks in the surface and then mark ridges around the mouth by stroking with your fingertips. Make two teeth using trimmings.

Unroll the covering around the cake

Pad the face with cream sugarpaste

Cut around the shape following the step picture

8 To make the scarf, roll out 340 g (12 oz) of red sugarpaste into an oval shape measuring 20 x 30 cm (8 x 12 in). Place on top of the skull's head with the longer length's excess on the side of the tied knot. Smooth the covering encouraging pleats and then pinch at the side to indent ready for the knot. To make the knot, stick the remaining red onto the indentation pinching gently to shape.

9 Roll 15 g (½ oz) of black modelling paste into a ball and press down to flatten. Cut the top straight and then stick the resulting patch over one eye. Roll a long thin sausage using the remainder, cut the ends straight and use for the eye patch tie.

10 For the skull and crossbones on the eye patch, thinly roll out white and cut two small strips 2.5 cm (1 in) in length and stick these crossed on the centre of the patch. Add a flattened ball to each end pressing each flat and then indent with the tip of a knife.

11 Roll 10 g (¼ oz) of white into a ball for the skull's eyeball and then stick on a flattened circle of brown with a small black circle for the pupil. Dilute red food colouring with a drop of water and then paint the veins at the back.

12 To make the skull's earring, thickly roll out white modelling paste and cut out a ring using the 2.5 cm (1 in) and 3 cm (1¼ in) circle cutters and then set aside to firm up a little before sticking in position using a little edible glue.

13 Stick pea-sized balls together over the cake board making the necklace. For coins, thinly roll out and cut 2.5 cm (1 in) circles for the gold coins, indenting around the edge of each by pressing the side of a cocktail stick into the surface. Cut 3 cm (1¼ in) circles for the silver coins.

14 To make the jewels, thickly roll out red and blue modelling paste and cut out a circle using the smaller circle cutter. To shape each jewel, evenly slice down at an outwards angle six times around the circle using a knife.

15 Dilute the brown food colouring with the water and paint a thin coat over the skull's face using the no.6 paintbrush. Paint the coins, necklace and earring using the gold and silver food colouring and then brush a little gold around the base.

Trumpet tower

What you will need

See pages 7 to 19 for recipes and techniques.

- 2 x 18 cm (6 in) & 2 x 10 cm (4 in) round cakes, each 6 cm (2½ in) depth
- 625 g (1 lb 6 oz/2¾ c) cake filling
- Icing (powdered) sugar in a sugar shaker

Sugarpaste
- 400 g (14 oz) green
- 900 g (2 lb) white

Modelling paste
- 315 g (11 oz) white
- 45 g (1½ oz) pale green
- 30 g (1 oz) black
- 10 g (¼ oz) red
- 5 g (just under ¼ oz) skin-tone

- Edible glue
- Black food colouring
- Pink and pale green powder food colouring

Equipment
- 30 cm (12 in) round cake board
- Large rolling pin
- Cake smoother
- Small plain bladed knife
- Serrated carving knife
- Palette knife
- Template (see page 124)
- Foam pieces or kitchen paper
- Length of food-safe dowelling (optional)
- Miniature circle cutter
- Six black food-safe flower stamens
- A few cocktail sticks
- No.2 sable paintbrush (for edible glue)
- No.3 sable paintbrush

An upside down Trumpet Lily makes a gorgeous fantasy home for these cute little character ladybirds.

Spread a thin crumb coat over the cake

1 Using a sprinkling of icing (powdered) sugar to prevent sticking, roll out the pale green sugarpaste to a thickness of 2–3 mm (¹⁄₈ in) and use to cover the cake board. Smooth the surface with a cake smoother and then trim excess from around the edge. Put aside to dry.

2 Trim the crust from each cake and level the tops. Cut a layer in each and then position the smaller cakes centrally on top of the larger cakes. Cut down and around the cake sculpting the sides so the surface is smooth. Round off the top of the cake and then slice down around the base so the cake narrows slightly.

3 Sandwich all layers together with cake filling and then spread a layer over the surface of the whole cake as a crumb coat and to help the sugarpaste stick. Position the cake centrally on the cake board.

tip

You may insert a food safe dowel down through the cake to help hold the layers in place. This is recommended if working in hot climates as the filling can soften causing the layers to slip.

4 Roll out 900 g (2 lb) of white sugarpaste and cut a strip the height of the cake and measuring 60 cm (24 in) in length. Dust with icing (powdered) sugar and then roll up opposite ends. Position this rolled up length of sugarpaste against the cake and unroll around it, trimming excess from the join at the top and smoothing closed. Rub the surface with a cake smoother.

5 There are six petals, three of each of the two templates (see page 124). Make the three thinner petals first, sticking each evenly around the cake. To make a petal, thinly roll out white modelling paste and cut out a petal shape. Use the rolling pin to lengthen further thinning out around the outside edge. Mark vein lines using the end of a paintbrush by stroking gently. Stick in position with the end curled up and supported with foam pieces or rolled up kitchen paper until dry. Make the three wider petals and roll the last petal up further exposing the door area.

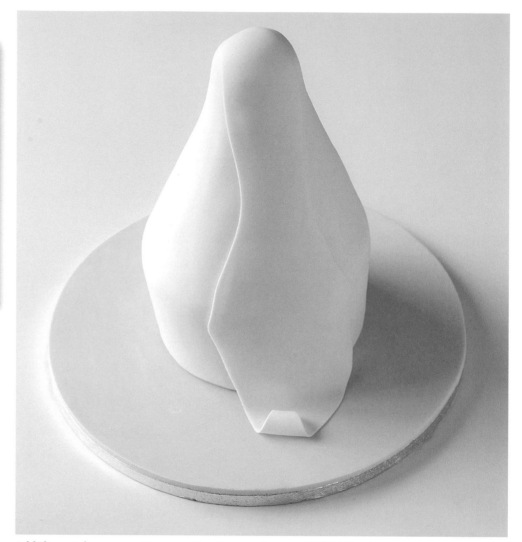

Add the petals one at a time, positioning evenly around the cake

Making the calyx

6 Cut out a doorway and three windows, removing the covering. Thinly roll out white trimmings and cut out a doorway and windows to fill the spaces. To make the steps, roll out white paste and cut a small strip, slice one third and place on top towards the back. Press down onto the centre of each to shape a dip in the steps.

7 For a shadow effect at the doorway and windows, dilute a little black food colouring with a few drops of water and then stipple some colour over the surface. Thinly roll out white and cut strips for the windowpanes and thicker strips for windowsills. Use trimmings to model the tiny flattened oval-shapes for the pathway.

8 Make the calyx using the step picture as a guide and the green modelling paste. To remove the join at the bottom of the stalk, rub gently with a little edible glue to blend in completely. Dust green powder colour around the base of the cake, along the centre of each petal and dust a little in each window and the doorway area.

Ladybirds

9 To make their bodies, split 15 g (½ oz) of black modelling paste into three pieces and roll into ball shapes, marking lines over the surface of one for the upturned ladybird's tummy. For their wings, split the red into three, roll into balls and then press down to flatten. Mark a line down the centre and then cut a small 'v' from the end of each.

10 Stick in position with one ladybird tummy up resting on the petal and the remaining two on the cake board with a few tiny flattened circles of black added to their wings for their markings. To make their legs, roll tiny sausages of black and bend one end round on each. Press down to flatten slightly making the feet.

11 To make their heads, split the skin-tone modelling paste into three pieces. Roll each into fat sausage shapes and then roll back and forth in the centre only rounding off each opposite end for the cheeks. Stroke down in the centre to flatten the mouth area and shape the chin by pinching gently. Indent their mouths using the miniature circle cutter pushed in at an upwards angle and then dimple the corners using a cocktail stick.

12 Using the remaining black, roll small oval-shapes, press each flat and then stick in place covering the back of their heads. Roll tiny black ball-shaped eyes with flattened circles of white and black for pupils and then roll tiny oval-shaped black noses. Brush a little red powder colour over each of their cheeks.

13 For the ladybird's antennas, moisten the bottom of each black stamen with a little edible glue and then push gently down in place, turning each out slightly.

tip

If you prefer to make your own antennas, roll tiny sausages of black modelling paste rounding off each end. Make a small hole in the ladybird's head. Leave the antennas to dry before carefully pushing down into place.

Detail of the ladybirds

Ladybird's head

45

Alien egg

What you will need

See pages 7 to 19 for recipes and techniques.

- 2 x 15 cm (6 in) dia. bowl-shaped cakes
- 450 g (1 lb/2 c) cake filling
- Icing (powdered) sugar in a sugar shaker

Sugarpaste
- 900 g (2 lb) cream

Modelling paste
- 450 g (1 lb) cream
- 90 g (3 oz) red
- 160 g (5½ oz) lime green
- 5 g (¼ oz) white
- Tiny piece of black

- Edible glue
- Brown liquid food colouring
- Lime green piping gel

Equipment
- 25 cm (10 in) petal-shaped cake board
- 1 x 10 cm (4 in) round cake card
- Large rolling pin
- Small plain bladed knife
- Serrated carving knife
- Palette knife
- Cotton thread
- Scissors
- Bone or ball tool
- No.2 sable paintbrush (for edible glue)
- No.4 sable paintbrush (for painting)

Even with the oozing green slime and gruesome globs of red, this alien is still scarily cute.

Roll the covering around the cake

Cut points into the top using scissors

1 Using the cream modelling paste, roll out and cover the cake board (see page 18, how to cover a cake board), taking the sugarpaste right over the sides and trimming excess from around the base. Mark the surface by indenting with your hands and then set aside to dry.

2 Trim the crust from each cake, level the tops and cut a central layer in each. Check the cake card is the same circumference as the bottom of the cake and trim if necessary. Using a little filling, assemble the cake onto the cake card and sandwich all layers together. Spread a layer over the surface to act as a coat to seal the cake and help the sugarpaste stick.

3 Roll out 45 g (1½ oz) of red sugarpaste and use to cover the top of the cake only. Measure the circumference of the cake using the cotton thread, cut to size and then spread out onto the work surface to use as a cutting guide. Roll out the cream sugarpaste into a strip measuring this length and cut 2.5 cm (1 in) higher than the height. Sprinkle with icing (powdered) sugar and gently roll up one side.

Place the covering against the cake and unroll around it, cutting excess from the join and smoothing closed.

4 Cut into points along the top edge using scissors. Smooth each point to thin and then turn out slightly. To texture the cake covering, press over the surface with your fingertips and then model different sized flattened oval-shapes using cream trimmings. Stick over the cake and smooth them in line with the cake surface. Position the cake centrally on the cake board.

Alien's head shape

Alien's hands

5 Dilute the brown food colouring until it reaches a translucent watercolour paint consistency. Brush over the surface of the cake letting it run down the sides and drip. Stipple excess over the cake board, making it darker around the bottom of the cake.

Alien

6 To model the alien's head, roll 115 g (4 oz) of lime green modelling paste into an oval shape and press down on one end to flatten. Indent the eye area using the bone or ball tool by pressing in with a circular motion. Smooth the outline underneath also.

7 Split the white modelling paste in half and use to make the oval-shaped eyes, adding two tiny oval-shaped black pupils onto the centre. Add two small tapering sausage shaped eyelids, smoothing the end of each in line with the surface at the outside edge.

8 Indent holes around the head by pressing in with the end of a paintbrush. Make three further holes, one for the antenna and then for ears either side of his head. Roll lots of tiny lime green

pieces for hairs and three thin sausage shapes, bending each around. Model three pea-sized ball shapes, press down and indent into the centre of each using the small end of the bone or ball tool and stick onto the thin sausage shapes making the antenna and ears, and then set aside. Stick the head in position on top of the cake, pushing down gently into the red covering.

9 Model different sized globs of red modelling paste and stick in position dripping around the cake and oozing out of the top.

Hands

10 Split the remaining lime green modelling paste in half and use to make the two hands. Using tiny pea-sized pieces first model the circular fingertips as before and set aside. To make a hand, roll a fat sausage shape and indent into the centre to round off the hand. Roll one end slightly longer for the forearm and press down on the opposite end ready to cut the fingers. Cut the thumb first on one side and then three slightly shorter cuts along the top to separate fingers. Roll each finger and the thumb longer by rolling gently and indent

along each for the joints. Roll the tips into points. Bend the fingers into position and stick on the circular fingertips. Stick in position at the top of the cake, each supported by the top edge of the cake covering.

11 When dry, stick the ears, antenna and hairs in position into the indented holes using a little edible glue to secure. Drip lots of lime green piping gel around the cake and pour some into the top of the egg allowing it to ooze out down the cake sides.

Back view

Frog prince

What you will need

See pages 7 to 19 for recipes and techniques.

- 1 x 20 cm (8 in) dia. bowl-shaped cake & 1 x 20 cm (8 in) round cake
- 450 g (1 lb/2 c) cake filling
- Icing (powdered) sugar in a sugar shaker

Sugarpaste
450 g (1 lb) pale blue
1.1 kg (2 lb 6¾ oz) lilac

Modelling paste
- 145 g (5 oz) lilac
- 115 g (4 oz) skin-tone
- 60 g (1 oz) dark yellow
- 45 g (1½ oz) green
- 45 g (1½ oz) pink
- Tiny piece of pale pink
- Tiny piece of black

- Edible glue
- Pink powder food colouring

Equipment
- 35 cm (14 in) round cake board
- 20 cm (8 in) round cake card
- Large rolling pin
- Small plain bladed knife
- Serrated carving knife
- Palette knife
- Miniature circle cutter (or No.18 PME piping tube (tip))
- 7 cm (2¾ in) and 2 cm (¾ in) circle cutters
- 1 x food safe plastic dowelling
- Cake smoother
- No.2 sable paintbrush (for edible glue)
- Cocktail sticks
- Dusting brush
- No.1 sable paintbrush (for painting)
- Miniature heart cutter

One of my favourite fairy tales, here's the beautiful Princess about to kiss her Prince Charming.

Pad the cake for the dress pleats

Cake board

1 Using the pale blue sugarpaste, roll out and cover the cake board (see page 18, how to cover a cake board). Stroke with your fingertip and indent with the circle cutters as a guide for the water ripples and then set aside to dry.

Cake

2 Trim the crust from each cake, level the tops and then cut a layer in each. Place the dome shaped cake on top of the round. Slice out small wedges of cake for the fabric pleats. Check the cake card is the same circumference as the cake and trim if necessary. Using a little filling, assemble the cake onto the cake card and sandwich all layers together. Spread a layer over the surface of the cake as a crumb coat to seal the cake and help the sugarpaste stick.

3 Using the lilac sugarpaste roll different sized long tapering sausages and stick onto the cake to make the fullness of the dress, adding more around the back of the cake. Roll out the remaining lilac sugarpaste and cover the cake completely, smoothing down and around the shape and trimming excess from around the base. Press the surface with a cake smoother to make the pleats more angled. Position the cake on the cake board, leaving plenty of space at the front.

Bodice

4 To make her bodice, roll 75 g (2½ oz) of lilac modelling paste into a ball and then pinch gently halfway to shape her waist. Place down on the work surface and indent the chest area by pressing in with your finger at the front and smooth a ridge. Cut the bottom straight. Stick a small flattened oval-shape of skin-tone into the chest area using a little edible glue and then stick onto the dress slightly towards the front. Push the dowelling down through the body to help support her leaving some protruding to help support her head.

Princess' face

Arms

5 Split 30 g (1 oz) of skin-tone modelling paste in half. To make an arm, roll one half into a short sausage and round off one end for the hand by pinching gently. Press the rounded end flat and make a cut for the thumb on one side no further than half-way. Make three further cuts along the top to separate fingers and stroke each gently to lengthen and round off. Push the thumb towards the palm from the wrist. To indent the elbow, gently pinch out at the back and indent at the front narrowing it slightly and then stick in position against the bodice. Repeat for the second arm, cutting the opposite thumb.

6 For sleeves, split 60 g (2 oz) of lilac modelling paste in half, roll into ball shapes and stick in position over the top of each arm. Add a little strip to the base of each pinching the edge to thin and frill and indent pleats at the top.

Face

7 Roll 75 g (2½ oz) of skin-tone modelling paste into a ball for her head. Indent in the centre by rolling your fingertip across and smooth to remove any imperfections. Pinch at the bottom to shape her chin. Roll a tiny teardrop shaped nose and stick in position. Mark nostrils by pressing in gently with the end of a paintbrush. For eyes, roll two tiny pea-sized balls of skin-tone and press down to flatten. Cut each straight along the bottom and stick in position.

Lips

8 Roll a small ball of pale pink modelling paste and indent into the centre with the end of a paintbrush. Mark lines radiating around the centre using a knife. Cut the shape angled at the top and sides and then stick in position. Edge the bottom of each eye with tiny

modelled sausages of black for eyelashes. Roll two tiny eyebrows using dark yellow, stick in position and texture with a knife. Brush a little pink powder colour over her cheeks for a blush. Push the head down onto the doweling securing at the base with edible glue.

Frog

9 To make the frog, roll 20 g (¾ oz) of green modelling paste into a ball and then roll in the centre to round off both ends, one slightly larger than the other. Pinch at the front of the smaller end to flatten the mouth area and then roll the knife across the surface to mark the mouth.

10 Using 5 g (¼ oz) of skin-tone modelling paste model as the body shape and then press down to flatten using a cake smoother. Stick the resulting patch onto the front of the frog's body smoothing the edge in line with the surface.

11 Indent two nostrils using the tip of a cocktail stick. Roll two tiny green balls and add two flattened circles of white and two black pupils to make eyes. For the legs, split 5 g (¼ oz) in half and roll

Bodice

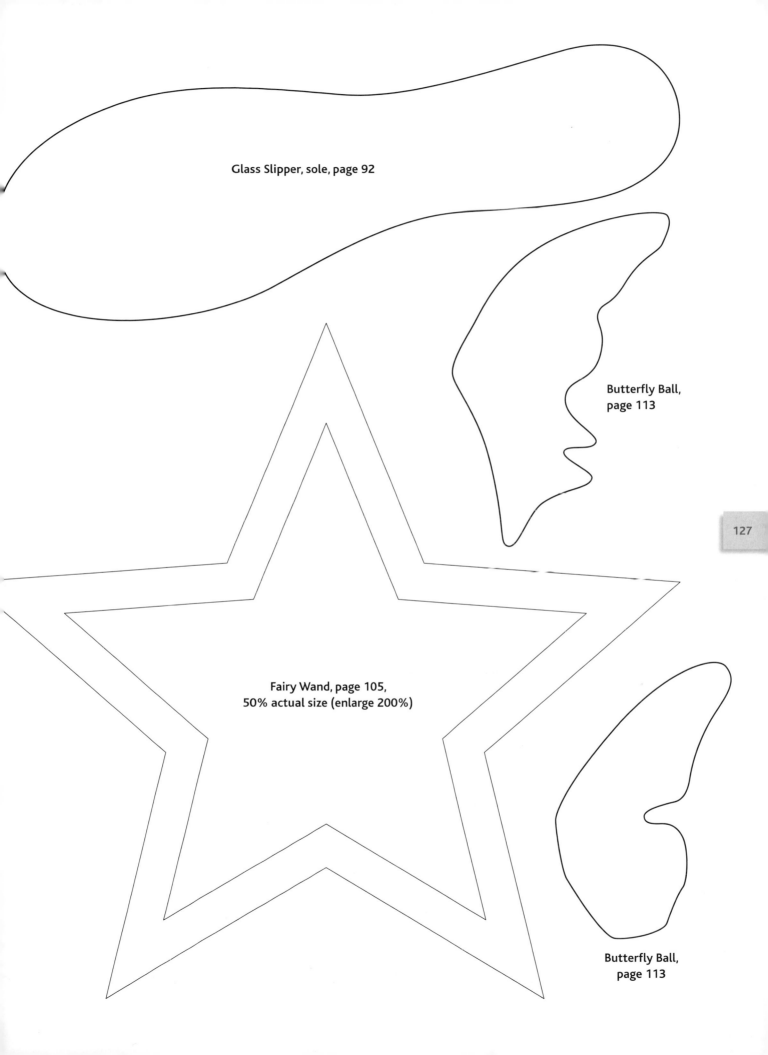

Glass Slipper, sole, page 92

Butterfly Ball,
page 113

Fairy Wand, page 105,
50% actual size (enlarge 200%)

Butterfly Ball,
page 113

Index

Shapes to build up the frog

into tapering sausage shapes, bending half way. For feet, roll small pea-sized teardrop shapes and cut into the point of each twice to separate and then stick in position at the end of each leg, turned slightly outwards.

12 For arms roll tapering sausage shapes rounding off the end of each slightly. Cut twice into the end and then stick the resulting arms in position either side of his body. Roll minute ball shapes and stick over the frog's back. Stick the frog into the Princess' hands resting against her dress.

13 To make the lily pad, roll out the remaining green and cut a circle with the larger circle cutter. Roll the paintbrush handle over the outside edge to thin and frill and then slice out a little smoothing the cut edge with your fingertip.

Hair

14 The hair is built up little by little using the dark yellow modelling paste. Shape into long different sized tapering strips and roll flat or press down with your palm to flatten. Stick in place building up the hair from the back of the head making smaller lengths framing her face.

Crowns

15 Roll out the pink modelling paste and cut a strip measuring 2.5 x 10 cm (1 x 4 in). Cut out circles from the top using the smaller circle cutter and then loop the strip around sticking the join closed. Use trimmings to cut tiny strips to edge the bottom of each cut out with one covering the join. Stick the crown on her head with little pink hearts decorating the top. Make the frog's crown using the miniature circle cutter and lilac modelling paste, turning it out slightly at the top.

Swags & Roses

16 To decorate the bottom of her dress, roll lilac trimmings into tapering sausages, press down to flatten slightly and then press the length of the paintbrush handle into the surface to indent pleats. Stick these in position with a tiny pink rose. To make a rose, roll a pea-sized pink ball then roll into a sausage shape at least 5 cm (2 in) in length. Press down to flatten and then using your fingertip stroke out a scalloped edge on one side. Roll this strip up with the scalloped edge uppermost and pinch at the bottom to help push out the centre. Stroke out the petals at the top and then stick the rose in position in between each swag.

Back view

Scary octopus

What you will need

See pages 7 to 19 for recipes and techniques.

- 2 x 23 cm (9 in) bowl-shaped cakes
- 450 g (1 lb/2 c) cake filling
- Icing (powdered) sugar in a sugar shaker

Sugarpaste
- 450 g (1 lb) bright green
- 900 g (2 lb) pale grey

Modelling paste
- 200 g (7 oz) pale grey
- 45 g (1½ oz) black
- 565 g (1 lb 4 oz) purple
- 5 g (just under ¼ oz) skin tone
- Tiny piece of brown
- 10 g (¼ oz) orange

- Edible glue
- Edible silver lustre powder

Equipment
- 35 cm (14 in) round cake board
- Large rolling pin
- Small plain bladed knife
- Serrated carving knife
- Palette knife
- Cake smoother
- 2.5 cm (1 in), 3.5 cm (1¼ in), 4 cm (1½ in), 5 cm (2 in), 6 cm (2½ in) and 9 cm (3½ in) circle cutters
- Food safe plastic dowel
- A few cocktail sticks
- No.2 sable paintbrush (for edible glue)

Surprisingly, an octopus has arms and not legs or tentacles. This angry looking giant octopus has his eight long arms wrapped tightly around his prey and doesn't look like he's letting go anytime soon!

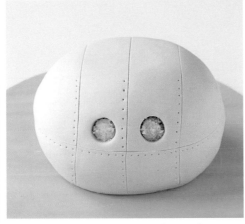

Cut out the portholes using the circle cutter   **Making the top of the submarine**

1 Using a sprinkling of icing (powdered) sugar to prevent sticking, roll out the green sugarpaste to a thickness of around 2–3 mm (⅛ in)and use to cover the cake board. Roll the rolling pin over the surface to indent ripples and then trim excess from around the edge. Reserve the trimmings and then put aside to dry.

2 Trim the crust from each cake and level the tops. Cut a layer in each cake and put together making a spherical. Trim either side of the cake to make it oval-shaped. Sandwich all layers together and spread a layer over the surface of the cake as a crumb coat to seal the cake and help the sugarpaste stick.

3 Roll out the pale grey sugarpaste to a thickness of 3-4 mm (⅛ in) and use to cover the cake completely, smoothing down and around the shape. Trim excess from around the base and smooth underneath. Position the cake centrally on the cake board.

4 Rub the surface with a cake smoother or use a 30 g (1 oz) ball of grey trimmings and rub over the surface in a circular motion to remove dimples. Using a knife, mark the lines by drawing the knife through the paste carefully, taking care not to cause the paste to pucker. Edge with holes indented with a cocktail stick.

5 Thickly roll out 35 g (1¼ oz) of pale grey modelling paste and cut a large circle using the 9 cm (3½ in) cutter. Cut a curve in one side using this cutter making a space for the black window area and then stick in position centrally on top of the submarine.

6 Roll a 90 g (3 oz) ball of black modelling paste and stick in position on the top of the submarine with a grey circle covering the top cut with the 6 cm (2½ in) circle cutter. Cut two more circles for the top using the 4 cm (1½ in) cutter and smooth the edges to round off. Stick in position and then mark the top of one with the 3.5 cm (1¼ in) cutter indenting holes as before.

7 To edge around the bottom of the black window, roll a thin sausage of pale grey and smooth to flatten slightly. Cut out four windows, two each on opposite sides of the submarine using the 2.5 cm (1 in) cutter. Thinly roll out black and fill the holes. Thinly roll out pale grey and cut hoops with the 2.5 cm (1 in) and 3.5 cm (1¼ in) cutters. Stick in position and then edge each with holes indented as before.

8 For the front of the submarine, cut out two circles using the 6 cm (2½ in) and 4 cm (1½ in) cutters smoothing the edges to round off as before. Stick in position and hold up for a few moments until secure.

9 For the back, roll a 25 g (¾ oz) sausage of pale grey and press down to flatten using a cake smoother. Bend it slightly to dip on one side and then using the large circle cutter cut out a curve on the opposite side. Moisten the rough surface of the cut with a little edible glue, wait for a few moments to become tacky and then stick in position across the back of the submarine, holding for a few moments until secure.

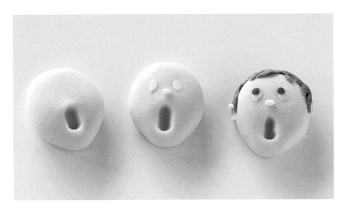

Modelling the head

10 To make the rudder, roll the remaining pale grey into a teardrop shape and press down to flatten slightly. Cut straight across the rounded end and then at an angle on one side and stick with the narrow end upright against the back.

11 Roll three quarters of the skin tone into an oval shape and press down to flatten slightly. Stick in place at the window and then open the mouth by pushing the end of a paintbrush into the mouth area and gently move up and down. Roll a tiny ball nose and two oval-shaped ears, indenting into the centre of each using the end of a paintbrush. Make two tiny white circles for eyes with even smaller circles of black for iris. Stick tiny teardrop shapes of brown over his head making his hair.

Shaping the octopus' head

12 Split the remaining skin-tone in half and use to make the hands. To make a hand, model a teardrop shape and press down to flatten slightly. Make a small straight cut on one side for the thumb cutting halfway. Make three further cuts along the top to separate fingers and then stroke each to lengthen and round off. Press into the centre of the palm to indent and then stick in position.

13 Push the dowel down through the cake at the back of the window leaving a little protruding at the top ready to help hold the Octopus' head in place. Roll a teardrop shaped head using 200 g (7 oz) of purple modelling paste and push down onto the dowel and stick in position resting on top of the submarine.

14 To indent the mouth, press the 4 cm (1½ in) circle cutter downwards into the paste and then use a paintbrush to widen each corner. Smooth around the top edge of the mouth to indent. Press into the eye area using your fingertip and stick two flattened circles of white for eyes with two small flattened circles for pupils. Roll two eyebrows, stick in place and then smooth just above to indent creating a cross look.

15 Put aside a tiny ball of purple for later and then split the remainder into eight pieces. Roll long tapering sausages to make the arms, sticking each in place as they are made curling around the submarine.

16 To make the fish, roll teardrop shapes and bend the pointed end round. Open the mouths as before making them slightly larger. Make eyes as before. Stick tiny patches over their backs using the remaining purple. For fins, model tiny teardrop shapes, press flat and then indent radiating lines using a cocktail stick.

17 Using the green trimmings, roll long thin sausages to make seaweed and stick tiny flattened pebbles over the cake board. Dust the board with silver lustre powder.

55

tip

When indenting the mouth, use a little water on the brush to help smooth the surface.

Sea palace

What you will need

See pages 7 to 19 for recipes and techniques.

- 1 x 18 cm (7 in) and 1 x 15 cm (6 in) round cakes, each 7 cm (2½ in) depth
- 450 g (1 lb/2 c) cake filling
- Icing (powdered) sugar in a sugar shaker

Sugarpaste
- 1.5 kg (3 lb 5 oz) pale blue

Modelling paste
- 200 g (7 oz) pale blue
- 115 g (4 oz) lime green
- 15 g (½ oz) peach
- 15 g (½ oz) skin-tone
- 30 g (1 oz) chestnut brown
- 20 g (¾ oz) yellow
- 30 g (1 oz) bright blue
- 30 g (1 oz) orange
- 20 g (¾ oz) purple
- Tiny piece black

- Edible glue
- Sugar stick or food-safe internal support
- Pink and lime green powder food colouring
- Edible sparkle powder and/or food-safe or edible glitter

Equipment
- 30 cm (12 in) round cake board
- 1 x 15 cm (6 in) and 1 x 18 cm (7 in) round cake cards
- Large rolling pin
- Small plain bladed knife
- Serrated carving knife
- Palette knife
- 3 x food safe plastic dowelling
- Ruler
- No.2 sable paintbrush (for edible glue)
- 2 x Templates (see page 124–125)
- Small piece of voile fabric or fine texture mat
- Dusting brush
- Cocktail sticks

A really pretty underwater scene with a gorgeous mermaid is a lovely choice for a birthday treat and would look spectacular on a sea inspired prettily decorated party table.

Roll the covering around the cake

Cake board

1 Using a sprinkling of icing (powdered) sugar to prevent sticking, roll out 450 g (1 lb) of pale blue sugarpaste to a thickness of around 2–3mm (⅛ in) and use to cover the cake board. Press the rolling pin into the surface to indent ripples and then set aside to dry. Trim excess from around the edge.

2 Trim the crust from each cake and level the tops. Cut a layer in each and then put the larger cake centrally on top of the smaller cake. Trim around the cake slicing away the bottom edge of the larger cake so the whole cake has sloping sides down to the bottom. Check the smaller cake card is the same circumference as the cake and trim if necessary. Using a little

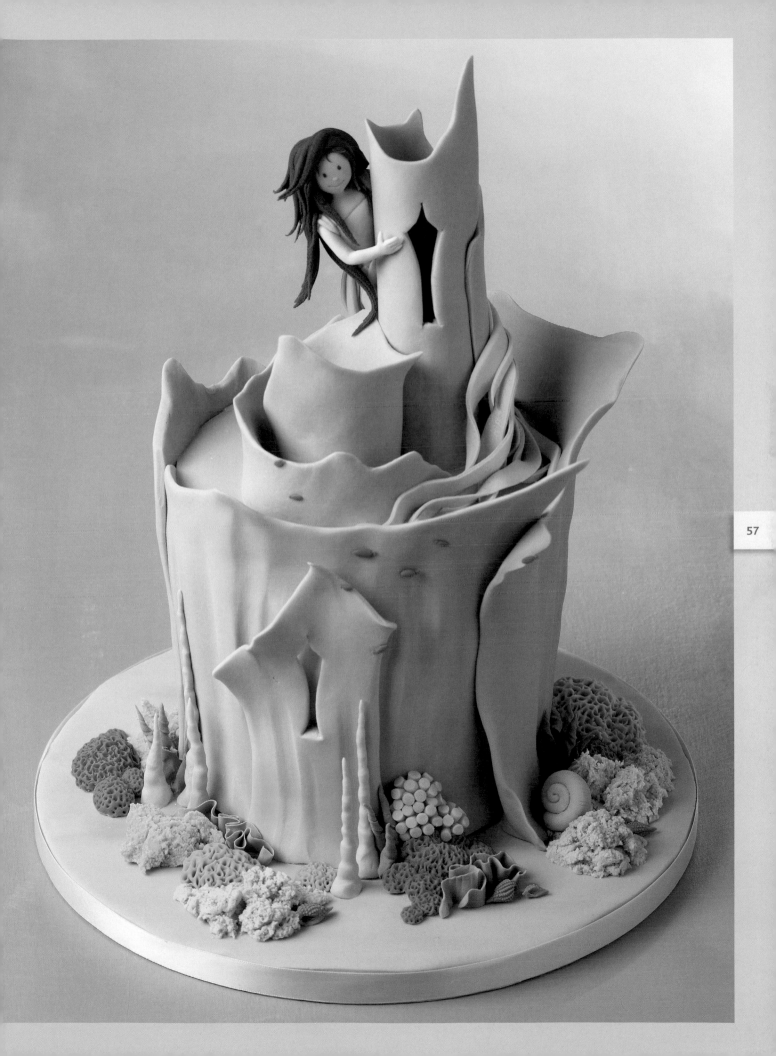

filling, assemble the cake onto the cake card and sandwich all layers together. Spread a layer over the surface of the cake as a crumb coat to seal the cake and help the sugarpaste stick.

3 To hold the weight of the towers and mermaid, push three dowels down through the cake, mark each level with the top, and then cut the same length even if they are all slightly different measurements. To cut plastic dowelling, simply score with a knife, hold directly underneath and either side and then snap to break. Cutting the dowels all the same measurement ensures the towers on the card will sit level on top of the cake.

4 Measure the height of the cake, roll out pale blue sugarpaste to a thickness of 3–4mm (1/8 in) and cut three sections one at a time, each slightly taller than the measurement and cut into different height points along the top. Roll the rolling pin over the surface to thin out the sugarpaste along the top only and mark vertical lines by pressing the rolling

pin along the surface. Brush edible glue around the top edge of the cake board, rework the crumb coat to ensure the surface is tacky and then position one piece at a time, securing the overlap with edible glue. Carefully lift the cake and position centrally on the cake board.

5 Check the larger cake card is the same circumference as the top of the cake and trim if necessary. Roll out 125 g (4½ oz) of pale blue sugarpaste and cover the card, trimming excess from around the edge and then place onto the top of the cake.

6 Roll out the trimmings and cut the front piece with window using the template and stick in position. Using the pale blue modelling paste roll out and cut the tall tower and spiral tower using the templates. Roll up the tall tower with the tube inside taking care when using the edible glue to secure the overlap that no glue gets onto the tube otherwise it will be difficult to remove. Lay the piece down to firm before standing upright and

Shapes for the mermaid's dress

removing the tube so the piece can dry completely. Spiral the second piece around and leave to dry upright.

Coral, seaweed, shells and fish

7 To allow for drying time make the coral next using all the different coloured modelling paste. The textures are created by cutting circles with piping tubes, indented with the end of a paintbrush and, for the fine texture, tearing apart modelling paste that has not been kneaded.

8 For the tall pale blue seaweed, roll long thin tapering sausage shapes and pinch along each to indent and then set aside to firm before positioning around the cake. To make the purple seaweed, shape different sized teardrop shapes and cut into the point, twisting each around pulling gently upwards. If they bend, lay flat for a few moments before sticking in place.

9 For the shells, roll the modelling paste into a spiral and mark along the surface with a knife. For the small pink shells, roll small teardrop shapes and make a hole for the opening at the full end. Pinch to narrow the full end slightly at the top and then roll the shell gently into the small piece of voile to texture the surface.

10 To make the fish, shape minute oval shapes and pinch one end to narrow for the tail. Make 10–20 tiny fish and stick in position dotted around the cake.

Mermaid

11 Stick the tower and spiral into position. Moisten around the back of the tall tower and allow the surface to become tacky. To make the mermaid's dress, model 30 g (1 oz) of lime green modelling paste into a long teardrop shape and pinch half way to narrow the waist. Press down gently and cut across the full end to straighten. Stick her dress in position wrapped around the back of the tower.

Spiral shaped top towers

12 Using the trimmings, roll two tiny flattened circles for her sleeves, indenting across the top of each using a cocktail stick. Roll the remaining lime green into long thin sausages and roll flat. Stick in position for her dress building up wrapped around the tall tower.

13 To make her chest area, roll one third of the skin-tone modelling paste into a fat sausage shape and gently pinch up a neck rolling gently to smooth. Cut the bottom straight so it sits neatly against the top of her dress. Push a cocktail stick down into the neck to make a hole ready for the internal support later, and then remove.

Arms

14 Make one arm at a time so they don't dry out before positioning. Split the remaining skin-tone modelling paste in half and set one piece aside for the head later. Split the second piece in half again and roll one into a sausage and pinch at one end to indent the wrist and round off the hand. Press down to flatten the hand slightly and then make a cut on one side for the thumb,

cutting no further than halfway the length of the hand. Make three further cuts along the top to separate fingers a little shorter than the thumb cut. Smooth the fingers to curve round and indent halfway along the arm for the elbow. Stick the arm in position securing against the tower. Make the second arm.

Head

15 Push the sugar stick or food-safe internal support down into the neck area leaving a little protruding ready to support the head. Set aside a tiny amount for her nose and then roll the remaining skin tone modelling paste into an oval shape and smooth the facial area flat. Push a cocktail stick into the bottom of the head to help hold whilst making the features. To mark her smile, push the side of a cocktail stick into the two opposite corners and then smooth inside using the tip of a paintbrush. Indent around the whole mouth by rolling the cocktail stick over the face towards the mouth causing excess, which creates the top and bottom lips. Stick on her tiny ball nose.

16 Using the black modelling paste, roll two minute black oval shapes and stick in position for eyes. Brush a little pink powder colour over her cheeks and across her lips. For hair, knead the chestnut modelling paste until soft, warm and stretchy when pulled. Gently pull out lengths from the paste until they're thin and tear and use these different sized lengths to create the hair.

17 Dust around the cake with lime green powder colouring and sprinkle with a little edible sparkle and/or food-safe glitter.

tip

If short of time, the hair can be piped with chestnut coloured royal icing. Use a paper piping bag with a small hole cut into the point and then pipe the strands over her head starting at the nape of her neck.

59

Back view

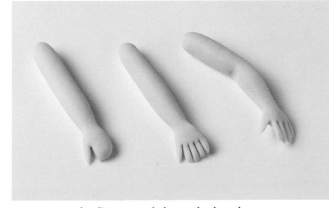

How to cut the fingers and shape the hand

Shark!

What you will need

See pages 7 to 19 for recipes and techniques.

- 1 x 20 cm (8 in) round and 1 x 20 cm (8 in) diameter bowl-shaped cake
- 450 g (1 lb/2c) cake filling
- Icing (powdered) sugar in a sugar shaker

Sugarpaste
- 370 g (13 oz) grey
- 100 g (3½ oz) white
- 115 g (4 oz) red
- Small piece of black
- 625 g (1 lb 6 oz) blue

Modelling paste
- 25 g (just over ¾ oz) skin-tone

- Edible glue
- 90 g (3 oz) clear piping gel

Equipment
- 30 cm (12 in) round cake board
- Large rolling pin
- Small plain bladed knife
- Serrated carving knife
- Palette knife
- A few cocktail sticks
- No.2 sable paintbrush (for edible glue)
- No.6 sable paintbrush

If this isn't gruesome enough, add another set of teeth just behind the first, he'll be even more terrifying and is sure to bring some squeals on serving, even more so if you add strawberry jam to the filling!

Trim the outline around the mouth area

1 Trim the crust from both cakes and level the tops. Cut layers in each and then place the bowl-shaped cake on top of the round cake. To shape the shark's nose, cut out the mouth area and use the trimmings to heighten the top of the cake. Trim around the bottom of the cake to round off.

2 Sandwich all layers together with cake filling and then spread a layer over the surface of the cake as a crumb coat and to help the sugarpaste stick. Add a little more around the nose area to fill any crevices making a smooth surface ready for the covering. If the layers slip, dip the palette knife into hot water.

3 Knead the grey sugarpaste until soft and pliable. Using a sprinkling of icing (powdered) sugar to prevent sticking, roll out to a thickness of 3–4 mm (1/8 in), lift and carefully place over the top of the shark covering his back and around the sides of his face. Trim away excess following the contours of his nose and cheeks. Trim excess from around the base.

4 Using your fingertip, push into the eye area either side to make holes for eyes, pushing gently towards the back of his head, and then stroke back and forth arching around the top to create the eyelid. For nostrils, push in and upwards using the paintbrush handle indenting two holes.

5 Roll out 75 g (2½ oz) of white sugarpaste and cut a strip for the white patch around his mouth. Indent lines across the top using the paintbrush handle. Split 5 g (just under ¼ oz) of white in half and use to make his eyes, sticking in place with a little edible glue.

6 Roll out the red sugarpaste and use to cover the mouth area, smoothing the covering carefully into the crevice. Push your fingertip along the top edge to indent holes ready for the teeth. To make the teeth, model little teardrop shapes and pinch the point to sharpen. Stick in place as each is made with slightly longer and more pointed teeth around the

sides. Stick two flattened circles of black onto his eyes for his pupils so the whites show around the back and sides only.

7 To make the arm, roll 5 g (just under ¼ oz) of skin-tone modelling paste into a sausage and pinch gently one end to round off for the hand. Press down on the hand to flatten slightly and then make a cut on one side for the thumb, cutting no further than halfway. Make three more slightly shorter cuts along the top for fingers and stroke each to round off and lengthen slightly. Push the thumb out and open the fingers. To shape the hand, press down onto the palm to indent.

Add the red covering smoothing gently into the mouth

tip

If short of drying time, use a food-safe internal support into each arm and leg to ensure they keep straight.

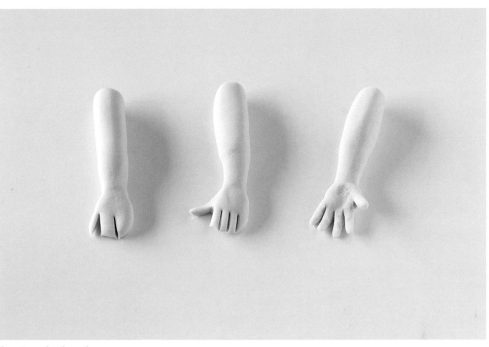

Shaping the hands

8 Split the remaining skin-tone modelling paste in half and use to make the two legs. To make a leg, roll one half into a fat sausage and bend over at the top pinching gently and taking care not to squeeze the toe area too flat. Pinch either side of the foot to narrow and lengthen and then push into the bottom of the foot and around the sides to indent the arch.

9 To cut the toes, make a small cut on one side for the big toe, stroke outwards and round off the tip by pressing slightly. Push the big toe back against the foot. Cut along the top of the foot to separate the remaining toes. Keep them tightly together and then stroke the top of each so they curve under slightly. Cut excess from the end of each leg and then set aside to dry.

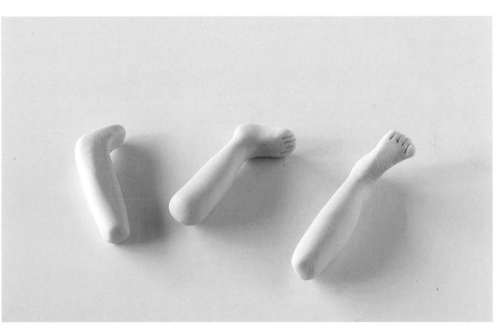

Shaping the legs and feet

10 Moisten around the cake board with edible glue. For the sea, roll out the blue sugarpaste and press over the surface of the cake board making the surface uneven. Cover the surface of the board completely trimming excess from around the edge. Smooth the joins closed by rubbing gently. Use a little edible glue to help stick if necessary.

11 Use blue trimmings to model all the teardrop shaped splashes. Stick the arm and legs in position. For the shiny water effect, paint a thin coat of clear piping gel over the surface, allow to set and then repeat until a high shine is achieved. Add a little to the shark's eyes and some splashes onto the feet.

tip

The piping gel's surface sets slightly but still remains sticky. Confectioner's glaze can be used as a substitute as this dries completely. Add 3-4 thin coats to achieve a high shine.

Acorn fairy

What you will need

See pages 7 to 19 for recipes and techniques.

- 1 x 20 cm (8 in) and 1 x 15 cm (6 in) round cakes
- 595 g (1 lb 5 oz) cake filling
- Icing (powdered) sugar in a sugar shaker

Sugarpaste
- 1.5 kg (3 lb 5 oz) pale blue

Petal paste
- 260 g (9 oz) pale golden brown

Modelling paste
- 25 g (just over ¾ oz) golden brown
- 30 g (1 oz) skin-tone
- 10 g (¼ oz) brown
- 15 g (½ oz) red/brown

Royal icing
- 60 g (2 oz)

- 1-2 tbsp white vegetable fat
- Edible glue
- Black food colouring
- Green, red and orange powder food colouring
- Edible gold lustre or sparkle powder

Equipment
- 35 cm (14 in) round cake board
- Large rolling pin
- Small plain bladed knife
- Serrated carving knife
- Palette knife
- Oak leaf cookie cutter or template (see page 125)
- A few cocktail sticks
- Bone or ball tool
- Leaf veiner (optional)
- No.2 sable paintbrush (for edible glue)
- Food-safe internal support (see page 19)
- No.3 (PME) piping tube (tip)
- No.0 (fine) sable paintbrush
- No.6 paintbrush or dusting brush
- Absorbant kitchen paper

Such a pretty fairy with her sweet smile, fiery red hair and gorgeous dress depicting the swirl of autumn oak leaves caught in a breeze.

Smooth a spiral of sugarpaste around the cake

1 Make all the leaves first allowing plenty of drying time. The dress has thirty leaves but I recommend you make a few more in case of breakage. To make a leaf, thinly roll out petal paste using a little white vegetable fat to prevent sticking. Rub a little white vegetable fat around the edge of the cutter and then cut out the leaf shape. I've included a leaf template so if you do not have a cutter, carefully cut around the shape using the point of a knife.

2 Using a rolling pin, roll gently over the cut out shape to thin out further concentrating more around the outside edge to thin and frill slightly and use a ball or bone tool to frill further by rubbing firmly but gently over the outside edge. Mark a line for the central vein using either a veiner tool or the end of a paintbrush. Mark slightly fainter vein lines from this central vein. Twist each leaf gently and curl up the corners and then set aside to dry. Repeat making all the leaves.

3 Trim the crust from each cake and level the tops. Cut a layer in each and then place the smaller cake centrally on top of the larger cake. Slice downwards around the cake cutting away the ridge in the centre making the surface smooth. Trim around the top to round off. Cut a small dip into the top where the fairy's body will sit later.

4 Sandwich all layers together with cake filling and assemble on the centre of the cake board using a little cake filling to secure. Spread a layer over the surface of the cake as a crumb coat and to help the sugarpaste stick.

5 To make the spiral effect around the cake, roll 400 g (14 oz) of pale blue sugarpaste into a long sausage tapering slightly at opposite ends and measuring no more than 90 cm (3 ft) in length. Carefully spiral around the cake twisting it out onto the cake board. Smooth along the top edge until in line with the surface of the cake to prevent slipping.

6 Roll out the pale blue sugarpaste and cover the cake and cake board completely, stretching out pleats and smoothing down and around the shape. Define the spiral underneath by smoothing with your fingertip and smooth more ridges spiralling around the cake board. Trim excess from around the cake board edge.

7 Next, make the fairy. Set aside a tiny piece of golden brown modelling paste for her lips later. To make her bodice, roll the remainder into a fat sausage and roll back and forth in the centre to round off opposite ends. Pinch out

one end to thin and frill. Lay the piece flat and press down at the opposite end to flatten the back and then push your fingertip into the front to indent the chest area. Using a little edible glue to secure, stick the bodice in position. Push the dowel or lolly stick down through her body and then remove.

8 For her chest and neck, roll a ball using 5g (just under ¼ oz) of skin-tone modelling paste and pinch up gently in the centre to make her neck. Push the food-safe internal support down through the neck and roll gently against the support cutting excess away at the top. Stick in position smoothing the neckline neatly into the space and then push the internal support down through the body and into the cake, leaving a little protruding at the top to help hold her head in place later.

9 Split 10 g (¼ oz) of skin-tone modelling paste in half and use to make the arms. To make an arm, roll one piece into a sausage measuring 6 cm (2¼ in). Note that this is not the finished length of the arm. Pinch gently around one end to round off for the hand and then press slightly flat. For the thumb, make a cut on one side cutting no further than halfway from the end of the hand to the wrist. Make three further slightly shorter cuts along the top to separate fingers. Roll each finger and thumb to lengthen and remove ridges and tap down on the tip of each to round off. To shape the hand, push the thumb down towards the palm from the base and stroke the fingers together bending them round slightly.

10 Moisten either side of the body with a little edible glue and leave to become tacky. To shape the elbow, pinch gently

halfway between the wrist and the shoulder bending gently. The total length of the arm should be 7.5 cm (2¾ in) from fingertip to shoulder. Make the second arm cutting the opposite thumb and then stick in position holding for a few moments until secure.

11 Put aside a tiny piece of skin-tone modelling paste for her nose later and roll the remainder into a ball for her head. Press down on the facial area to flatten slightly and pinch gently at the bottom to shape her chin.

12 Roll a tiny tapering oval-shape using the remaining golden brown, press flat and then stick onto her face for her mouth. To shape the lips, indent the centre by cutting with a knife, curving up the line slightly at the outer edges. Push into the centre with the end of a paintbrush to shape the lips and indent

Indent lines around the cake by smoothing with your fingertips

at the top to define the bow. To create dimples, indent the corners of the mouth using a cocktail stick.

13 Stick a tiny ball nose in position and indent nostrils using the end of a paintbrush. Push the head gently onto the internal support and secure at the bottom with a little edible glue.

14 To make the acorn hat, roll the brown modelling paste into a ball and pinch to hollow out stroking the outside edge to neaten. Pinch up at the top to create a stalk. Check to see if the hat fits properly and if it does stick in position with a little edible glue. If the hat is sitting too high on the head then hollow out further. Indent over the surface using the piping tube pushed in at an angle.

15 To make the hair, roll different sized sausages of red/brown modelling paste and press each to flatten slightly. To make the ripples, indent the surface by pressing along the surface with the paintbrush handle. Add a little blush to her cheeks using the red powder food colouring.

16 Dilute a little black food colouring with a drop of water. Using the fine paintbrush, paint her eyes. Paint a small oval-shaped pupil first, and then the eyelid around it, ensuring the eyelid line touches the pupil in the centre. Leave a small, unpainted area on each eye for the highlight. Paint fine eyelashes, three on each eye on the outside corners only. Paint fine arched lines above each eye for eyebrows, taking care not to make them too heavy.

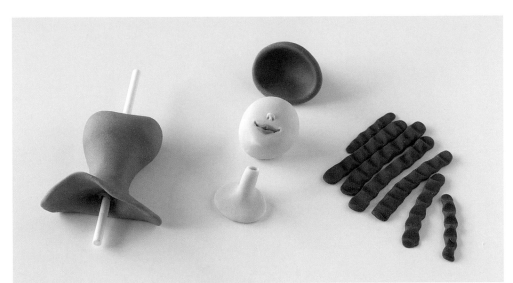

Use a food-safe support to help hold her in place

17 Using the powder colours, sprinkle a little of each onto kitchen paper and then dust the leaves all slightly differently.

18 Using dabs of royal icing, stick the leaves in position around the cake, building up around the top of her skirt to create fullness. Dust around the leaves and the fairy with gold lustre powder to give a pretty sparkle.

tip

If you want to set the powder colour on the leaves, hold each dusted leaf near a steaming kettle of water taking care not to get too close. Steam each leaf for around 5–10 seconds or until a slight sheen appears. Try not to touch the damp surface otherwise the colour will lift off onto your hands.

Dust the leaves with powder colour

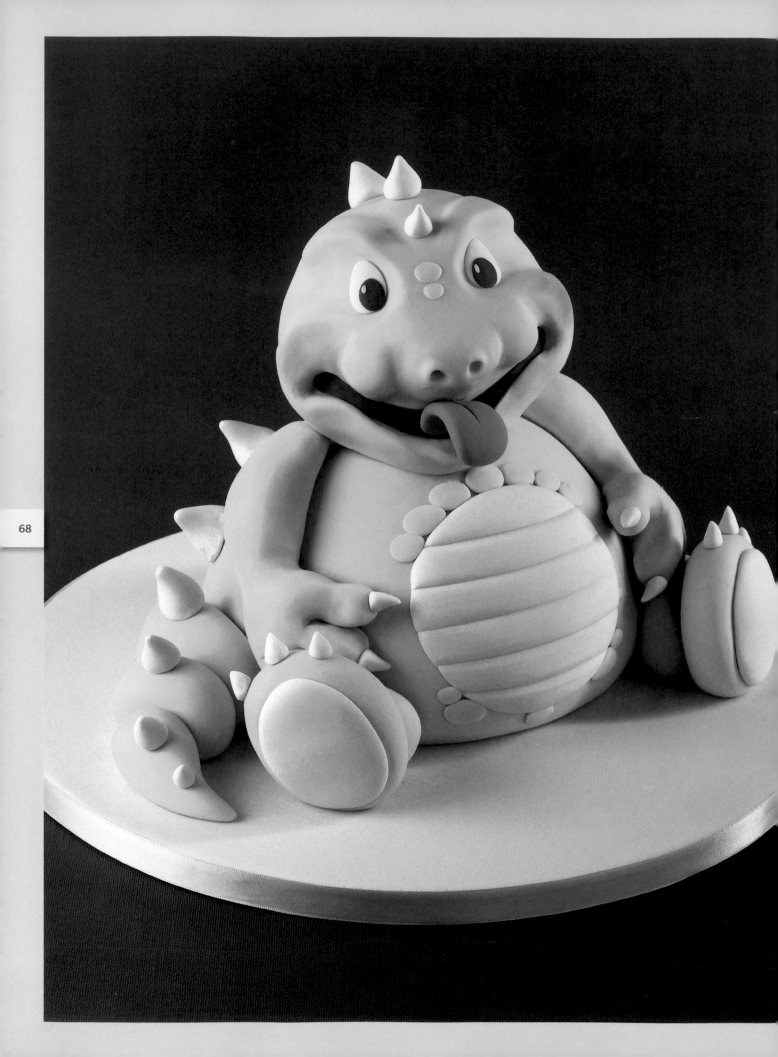

Baby dinosaur

What you will need

See pages 7 to 19 for recipes and techniques.

- 1 x 20 cm (8 in) round cake, 1 x 20 cm (8 in) and 2 x 12 cm (5 in) bowl-shaped cakes
- 625 g (1 lb 6 oz/2¾c) cake filling
- Icing (powdered) sugar in a sugar shaker

Sugarpaste
- 595 g (1 lb 5 oz) yellow
- 1.5 kg (3 lb 5 oz) green
- 5g (just under ¼ oz) black
- Small piece of white
- 10 g (¼ oz) pink

- Edible glue

Equipment
- 35 cm (14 in) round cake board
- Large rolling pin
- Small plain bladed knife
- Serrated carving knife
- Palette knife
- A few cocktail sticks
- Length of food-safe dowel
- No.2 sable paintbrush (for edible glue)
- 9 cm (3½ in) circle cutter
- Ruler

I nearly made a butterfly resting on this cheeky dinosaur's tongue, ready for his tea, but decided that could be a little too gruesome for some little ones.

Add the tail, curling it around the front

1 Using a sprinkling of icing (powdered) sugar to prevent sticking, roll out 450 g (1 lb) of yellow sugarpaste to a thickness of around 2–3 mm (⅛ in) and use to cover the cake board. Trim excess from around the edge and then put aside to dry.

2 Trim the crust from each cake and level the tops. To shape the body, place the large bowl-shaped cake on top of the round cake cutting a layer in each.

To make the head, place the two smaller bowl shaped cakes together making a spherical. Sandwich all layers together using cake filling keeping the body and head separate. Spread a crumb coat layer over the surface of both the body and head to seal the cakes and help the sugarpaste stick.

3 Cover the body first using 595 g (1 lb 5 oz) of green sugarpaste, smoothing and stretching down and around

the shape. Trim excess from around the base and then position on the cake board slightly to one side to allow room for his tail. Roll a 30 g (1 oz) ball of green, dust with icing (powdered) sugar and then use as a cake smoother by rubbing gently over the cake surface. Push the dowel down through the body leaving some protruding at the top to help hold the head in place later, taking care that it is not too long for the height of head.

Facial features

Smooth the covering to define facial features

tip

If you want a sweet and innocent expression instead of his devilish look, smooth the eyebrows flatter between his eyes.

4 Pad out the face as the step picture using 45 g (1½ oz) of green sugarpaste. Roll out 315 g (11 oz) and use to cover the head. Press gently around the facial features and then stretch out pleats in the covering and smooth downwards. Trim excess but ensure the whole cake is covered completely.

5 To define the facial features, smooth around the shapes using your fingertip. Indent nostrils with the end of a paintbrush. Stick the head in position using a little edible glue to secure at the base.

6 Put aside a minute piece of white sugarpaste and then use the remainder to make two oval-shaped eyes. Add two black pupils and then roll a tiny white highlight for each eye. For his mouth, roll a long thin sausage of black sugarpaste and then roll thinner at opposite ends. Press down to flatten and then stick into position smoothing gently in line with the surface of the covering.

7 Split 160 g (5½ oz) of green sugarpaste in half. To make the tail, first roll one

half into a ball and press down against the base of the dinosaur securing with a little edible glue. Split the remaining piece in half and roll another ball for the tail and a pointed teardrop shape for the tip.

8 To make the legs, split 90 g (3 oz) of green in half and roll into two ball shapes. For feet, split 175 g (6 oz), roll into ball shapes and press down to flatten slightly. Stick the legs and feet in position securing with a little edible glue.

9 To make the arms, put aside 10 g (¼ oz) of green and then split the remainder in half. Roll one half into a fat sausage shape and then roll back and forth one third from one end to indent and narrow the wrist. Press down the rounded end to flatten slightly and then make three cuts for his fingers. Narrow between each finger by pinching gently, rounding off the tips. Make the second arm and stick each in position using a little edible glue.

10 To make his tummy patch, thinly roll out yellow sugarpaste and cut a circle with the circle cutter. Indent

lines across the surface using a ruler and then smooth around the edge. Using the remaining green, model flattened oval shapes for scales.

11 For his feet, split 35 g (1¼ oz) of yellow in half and roll two oval shapes. Press down to flatten and then stick onto the bottom of each foot, smoothing around the outside edge of each to round off. With the remaining yellow, roll fat teardrop shapes graduating in size and use to edge his back, each foot and fingertips.

12 Moisten the mouth area with a little edible glue and leave to become tacky. To make the tongue, roll the pink sugarpaste into a teardrop shape and press down to flatten slightly. Using a knife, make a small indentation from the pointed end down to halfway and smooth gently to soften. Curve the tongue slightly and then stick in position holding for a few moments to secure. To finish, brush a little pink powder colour over his cheeks to give him a blush.

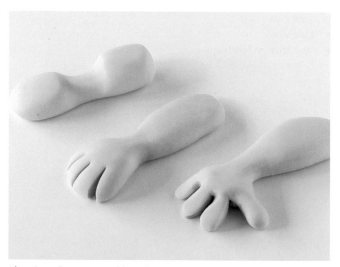

Shaping the arm and hand

Princess castle

What you will need

See pages 7 to 19 for recipes and techniques.

- 3 x 15 cm (6 in) round cakes each 5 cm (2 in) depth
- 450 g (1 lb/2 c) cake filling
- Icing (powdered) sugar in a sugar shaker

Sugarpaste
- 1.4 kg (3 lb 1½ oz) white

Modelling paste
- 800 g (1 lb 12 oz) white
- 45 g (1½ oz) pink
- 315 g (11 oz) dark pink
- 10 g (¼ oz) skin-tone
- 10 g (¼ oz) pale yellow
- 10 g (¼ oz) blue
- Tiny piece each of dark yellow and black

- Edible glue
- Edible silver colouring
- Sugar stick or food-safe internal support
- Pink and pale blue powder food colouring
- Edible sparkle powder and/ or food-safe or edible glitter

Equipment
- 25 cm (10 in) round cake board
- 2 x 15 cm (6 in) round cake cards
- Large rolling pin
- Small plain bladed knife
- Serrated carving knife
- Palette knife
- 3 x food safe plastic dowelling
- Cotton thread
- Ruler
- Cake smoother
- No.2 sable paintbrush (for edible glue)
- Template (see page 125)
- Dusting brush
- No.1 sable paintbrush (for painting)

Every little girl will love this gorgeous fairy tale castle with the elegant towers stretching into the clouds and a pretty little princess playing with her bluebird friends.

Unroll the covering around the cake

Cake board

1 Using 400 g (14 oz) of white sugarpaste, roll out and cover the cake board (see page 18, how to cover a cake board). Press the rolling pin into the surface to indent ripples and then set aside to dry.

Cake

2 Trim the crust from each cake, level the tops and then cut a central layer in each. Place one layer on top of each other. Trim around the cake so the sides slope inwards centrally. Keep the cake surface as smooth as possible. Check the cake card is the same circumference as the cake and trim if necessary. Using a little filling, assemble the cake onto the cake card and sandwich all layers together. Spread a layer over the surface as a crumb coat to seal the cake and help the sugarpaste stick.

Central tower

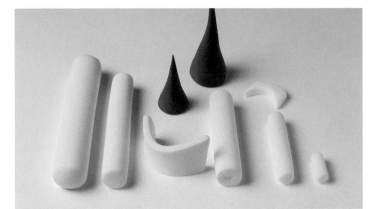

Allow the taller towers to dry before positioning

3 Push three dowels down through the cake, mark each level with the top, and then cut the lowest measurement if they are not the same. To cut plastic dowelling, simply score with a knife, hold directly underneath and either side and then snap to break. Cutting the dowels all the same measurement ensures the towers on the card will sit level on top of the cake.

4 Measure the circumference of the cake using a length of cotton thread and then lay out across the work surface to use as a cutting guide. Measure the height of the cake plus 2 cm (¾ in). Roll out the remaining white sugarpaste to a thickness of 3–4 mm (¹⁄₈ in). Cut a strip to cover the sides of the cake using these measurements. Smooth along the top edge to thin out and then dust with icing (powdered) sugar and gently roll up one side. Place the sugarpaste against the cake and unroll carefully around it, smoothing upwards to prevent it sinking and keeping the bottom in line with the base of the cake. Trim away excess at the join and rub gently to close with a little edible glue.

5 Roll a golf-ball sized ball of sugarpaste and rub gently over the cake surface in a circular motion; this will act as a smoother and remove any imperfections. Cut out the doorway at the front of the cake using the template. Smooth around the doorway to soften the edge. Thinly roll out white sugarpaste and cut a piece to fit the doorway. Place the cake centrally on the cake board securing with a dab of edible glue.

Towers

6 Check the second cake card is the same circumference as the top of the cake and trim if necessary. Roll out white modelling paste and cover the card.

Use a food-safe internal support for her head

7 To make the central tower, roll 135 g (4¾ oz) of white modelling paste into a fat sausage shape and indent around the centre to narrow slightly. Press down at either end to flatten and then set aside to dry.

8 For the towers, roll different sized sausage shapes in differing lengths between 6 cm (2½ in) to 18 cm (7 in) and set all aside flat down to dry. Roll the cake smoother gently back and forth over the surface to ensure a neat smooth sausage shape without any finger marks. Roll out and cut strips for the bridges and walls that will connect all the towers set aside.

9 Make all the towers attached to the side of the cake next, using a little glue to secure in place. Paint all the windows and doorway with a little edible silver colouring. Edge the bottom of each window with a little white strip of modelling paste making windowsills.

10 Set aside a tiny amount of white for later and then use the remainder to make all the cloud shapes, indenting around the edge of each using the back of a knife. Stick all the towers, bridges and walls in position.

Princess

11 To make the princess, first roll 35 g (1¼ oz) of pink modelling paste into a teardrop shape for her skirt and press down on the full end to flatten slightly. Smooth pleats into the surface using your fingertips and cut the top straight for her waist. Using 2 g/½ oz of pink, model two tiny ball puffed sleeves and set aside for later. Roll the remainder into a teardrop shape and press down on the centre to push up excess for her chest area. Cut both top and bottom straight and stick into position on top of the skirt.

12 For arms, use pea-sized amounts of skin-tone modelling paste for each, making one at a time. Roll into a sausage and round off the end for the hand. Press the hand down to flatten slightly and then make a cut on one side no further than half way for the thumb. Make three more cuts along the top, slightly shorter than the thumb cut and ensuring they are straight. Stroke the fingers and thumb gently to lengthen and then bend round for a natural pose. Make a small indent for the elbow and stick in position holding for a few moments until secure. Repeat for the second arm.

13 For her neck and chest area, roll a tiny ball of skin-tone and pinch up her neck, rounding it off gently. Make a small hole by pushing the tip of a cocktail stick into the neck ready for the internal support and then remove. Press down to flatten the bottom or cut straight and then stick in position on top of her bodice. Stick the two puffed sleeves in position covering the join at each shoulder. Push the sugar stick or food-safe internal support inside her neck leaving a little protruding to help hold her head in position later.

14 Thinly roll out dark pink modelling paste and using the template cut out the back of the dress, marking pleats with a paintbrush handle pressed gently into the surface and then stick in position.

15 Next, make her head using 2 g ($^1/_{16}$ oz) of skin-tone modelling paste. Roll into a ball and press down on the facial area to flatten slightly. Pinch at the bottom to shape the chin, making it slightly

pointed. Make a hole in the bottom using a cocktail stick and remove.

16 Model her face with minute pieces of modelling paste. Ensure you pinch off the tiniest amounts otherwise the features will be too heavy. If you prefer you may wish to paint the features with liquid food colouring and a very fine paintbrush. Stick her head in position securing with a little edible glue.

17 Using the remaining dark pink modelling paste, model all the pointed roofs, flattening each at the base so they sit level on top of each tower and secure with a little edible glue. Stick all the clouds into position. Thinly roll out dark pink trimmings and cut ribbons for the princess' dress.

18 For the Princess' hair, model long thin flattened teardrop shapes of pale yellow modelling paste and stick in position over her head building up the hairstyle and curling the ends round. Model a tiny cloud shaped crown and curve round slightly. Add a little blush to her cheeks using pink powder colour.

Birds

19 To make the birds, model teardrop shapes for their bodies and cut into the point repeatedly curling up the ends. Roll ball-shaped heads and stick in position on top of each body. For wings, roll pea-sized amounts of blue into teardrop shapes and press down flat. Mark the surface with a cocktail stick tearing gently along the bottom and then stick in position. Model a tiny teardrop shape for each head.

Shapes to make a bird

20 To make the beaks, roll minute sausage shapes of dark yellow tapering each end to a point. Flatten slightly then indent across the centre so the piece can fold easily. Use white and black modelling paste to make the eyes and eyelashes as before.

21 Dust blue powder colouring around the base of the cake making the colour deeper on the inside and fade out towards the cake board edge. To create a pretty sparkle, dust the cake with edible sparkle powder and/or food-safe or edible glitter.

Back view

Spider trap

What you will need

See pages 7 to 19 for recipes and techniques.

- 3 x 18 cm (7 in) square cakes (each 7 cm/2½ in depth)
- 450 g (1 lb/2c) cake filling
- Icing (powdered) sugar in a sugar shaker

Sugarpaste
- 1.6 kg (3 lb 8½ oz) dark lilac
- 115 g (4 oz) black

Modelling paste
- 90 g (3 oz) dark lilac
- 175 g (6 oz) black
- 10 g (¼ oz) white

- Edible glue
- Sugar sticks or food-safe internal supports
- Edible sparkle powder and/ or food-safe or edible glitter

Royal Icing
- 60 g (2 oz) dark lilac

Equipment
- 30 cm (12 in) round cake board
- 1 x 15 cm (6 in) square cake card
- Large rolling pin
- Small plain bladed knife
- Serrated carving knife
- Palette knife
- Ruler
- Cake smoother
- No.2 sable paintbrush (for edible glue)
- Template (see page 126)
- 2 cm (¾ in) and 3 cm (1¼ in) circle cutters
- 1 x food safe plastic dowelling
- Dusting brush
- Paper piping bag
- No.1.5 (PME) plain piping tube (tip)

This gorgeously gruesome design is certain to give someone the heebie-jeebies!

Covering sides

Cover roof last

1 Using 450 g (1 lb) of dark lilac sugarpaste, roll out and cover the cake board (see page 18, how to cover a cake board). Press the rolling pin into the surface to indent ripples and then set aside to dry.

2 Trim the crust, level the tops and then cut a layer in each cake. Position one on top of each other. To shape the roof, first measure across the top of the cake and mark a central line. Slice down from this mark either side, cutting down one third from the top. Trim opposite sides of the cake to slope gently inwards and then back outwards down to the base.

3 Check the cake card is the same size as the cake and trim if necessary. Using a little filling, assemble the cake onto the cake card and sandwich all layers together. Spread a layer over the surface of the cake as a crumb coat to help the sugarpaste stick.

4 Using dark lilac sugarpaste, roll out to a thickness of 3-4mm and cover each side of the cake, covering one side at a time. Cover the two opposite sides first and then the front and back, securing joins with edible glue. Rub the joins gently to remove, if they are stubborn then make a feature by cutting some cracks along the surface.

Roof

5 Roll out the remaining dark lilac sugarpaste and cut a piece slightly larger than the roof. Carefully lift and place on top of the cake. Use the cake smoother to remove any dimples in the surface and push along the edge to straighten any distortion.

6 Cut out the doorway and large crack in the side of the cake using the templates, removing the covering. Thinly roll out black sugarpaste and cut pieces to fill the spaces. Mark further cracks around the whole cake. Using the dark lilac sugarpaste trimmings, model the different sized rocks and oval shaped stones, sprinkle the rocks around the base of the cake and stick the stones to the cake surface to give texture and help hide any imperfections.

Chimney

7 Using the dark lilac modelling paste, roll into a sausage shape and push the dowel down through the centre leaving around 10 cm (4 in) protruding from one end. Press down with a cake smoother to flatten and then turn and repeat to gain the sharp edges. Smooth along the centre to narrow and then cut away each end making the end that rests against the roof slightly angled. Push the dowel down through the cake securing the base of the chimney with a little edible glue. Roll out trimmings and cut out the door arch.

Spiders

8 Make all the different sized spiders next, all with different sized bodies and heads.

Indent their grins with the circle cutters pushed in at an upwards angle. Use a sugar stick or food safe internal support to help hold each head in position. For legs, roll long thin tapering sausage shapes, bend near the top of the fuller end and lay flat to dry. When ready to assemble, make a small hole in the spider's body to help hold each leg in place with a little edible glue to secure.

9 Cut tiny strips for teeth, marking lines across with the back of a knife. Roll tiny white teardrop shapes for fangs. Model white oval shaped eyes with black pupils added to the bottom of each and then top each eye with a tiny sausage of black modelling paste applied at an angle to give an evil look.

Finial

10 Roll three tiny sausages of black modelling paste and spiral the top of each round. Stick two together smoothing the join closed and then stick the last one at the top. Lay flat to dry completely before securing at the front of the roof with a pea-sized piece of dark lilac modelling paste to hold it in place. Roll small balls of black modelling paste and use for the roof supports.

Web

11 Using the royal icing and the piping tube, pipe all the different sized spider webs around the cake. Lift the royal icing as you loop the pattern to gain a smooth piped line. Stick the spiders in position. Dust with edible sparkle powder and/or food-safe glitter.

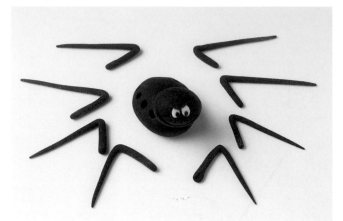

Leave the legs to dry before positioning

Pipe the web frame first and then the spiral

Side view

Flower fairy

What you will need

See pages 7 to 19 for recipes and techniques.

- 1 x 15 cm (6 in) & 2 x 10 cm (4 in) round cakes
- 565 g (1 lb 4 oz/2½c) cake filling
- Icing (powdered) sugar in a sugar shaker

Sugarpaste
- 1.25 kg (2 lb 12 oz) pink

Modelling paste
- 115 g (4 oz) pink
- 30 g (1 oz) blue
- 285 g (10 oz) white
- 25 g (just over ¼ oz) skin-tone
- 45 g (1 ½ oz) pale pink
- 45 g (1 ½ oz) pale blue
- Tiny piece of black
- 90 g (3 oz) yellow

- Edible glue
- Yellow and pink powder food colouring

Equipment
- 30 cm (12 in) round cake board
- 2 x 10 cm (4 in) round cake cards
- Large rolling pin
- Small plain bladed knife
- Serrated carving knife
- Palette knife
- Cake smoother
- Ruler
- 6 lengths of food-safe dowelling
- Small piece of card
- Assorted flower cutters
- 1.5 cm (½ in) heart shaped cutter
- Miniature star and heart cutters
- A few cocktail sticks
- No.2 sable paintbrush (for edible glue)
- No.6 sable paintbrush
- Foam sheet

This pretty bright pink castle with a gorgeous multi-coloured funky fairy would make a stunning centrepiece on the party table.

Indent windows with a piece of folded card

1 Using a sprinkling of icing (powdered) sugar to prevent sticking, roll out 400 g (14 oz) of pink sugarpaste to a thickness of 2–3 mm (¹⁄₈ in) and use to cover the cake board. Smooth the surface with a cake smoother and then trim excess from around the edge. Remove any excess icing (powdered) sugar by rubbing a small ball of pink sugarpaste over the surface and then set aside to dry, preferably overnight.

2 Trim the crust from each cake and level the tops. Cut a layer in each cake and then sandwich back together with cake filling. Due to shrinkage during baking, check that the small cake cards are the same circumference as the smaller cakes and if needed trim to fit. Place the smaller cakes on the cake cards securing with a dab of cake filling. Position the larger cake on the cake board, slightly towards the back using a little cake filling.

3 Roll out 300 g (10½ oz) of pink sugarpaste to a thickness of 3–4 mm (¹/₈ in) and cut a strip measuring the height of the cake and 50 cm (20 in) in length. Dust with icing (powdered) sugar and then roll up carefully. Position the end against the cake on the cake board slightly to the side at the front where the dress will be and unroll the paste around the cake. Trim excess from the join and close with edible glue.

4 Using a small piece of folded card, indent the slit windows around the sides of the cake, opening slightly for the graduation. Roll out 115 g (4 oz) of pink and use to cover the top of the cake, trimming carefully to keep a neat sharp edge so the castellation sits well.

5 So the top tower is supported well, push three dowels centrally down through the cake on the cake board taking care that they do not exceed a 10 cm (4 in) circumference. Mark each carefully level with the top, remove and place down on the work surface evenly side by side. Score all the dowels at the lowest mark so they are exactly the same height. Snap to break holding either side of the scored line. Insert again into the cake until level with the surface.

6 Dowel one of the smaller round cakes so the second smaller cake sits on top resting on the dowels prior to covering. Cover this double height cake using 340 g (12 oz) of pink sugarpaste for the sides and the remainder for the top and then position on top of the larger cake. Mark windows as before.

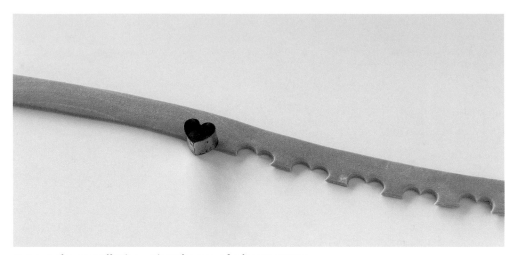

Cut out the castellation using the top of a heart cutter

7 Roll out the pink modelling paste and cut a strip to fit the circumference of the top edge of the bottom tier, 2 cm (¾ in) in depth. Moisten around the top edge with a little edible glue and leave to become tacky. To make the castellation, cut evenly along the top of the strip using the top of the large heart shaped cutter. Lift the strip carefully so not to tear and position around the top edge of the cake smoothing gently in place. Make the castellation for the top tier.

8 Using 10 g (¼ oz) of pink, model tiny sausages to trim the windows and model tiny ball shapes to edge along the bottom of each castellation.

9 To make the fairy wings, knead 20 g (¾ oz) each of pink and blue modelling paste together until marbled. Split in half and then roll out fat teardrop shapes encouraging the wavy top edge on each. Stick in position onto the top tier of the cake leaving a small space in between each. Edge each wing with flattened sausages curled around using pale pink and pale blue modelling paste.

10 Moisten between the wings and down the front of the cake with a little edible glue and leave to become tacky. To make her dress, roll 175 g (6 oz) of white modelling paste into a fat sausage. Roll back and forth 2 cm (¾ in) from the top to round off her chest and narrow her waist.

11 Roll the rolling pin down over the skirt so it gradually gets thinner down to the bottom. Also roll out either side to widen the skirt. Cut the top of her bodice straight and then stick the dress in position holding for a few moments to secure.

12 To make her chest and neck area, roll 5 g (just under ¼ oz) of skin-tone modelling paste into a fat sausage and pinch up centrally on one side rolling gently back and forth to make her neck. Lay this piece down on the work surface and cut straight across the bottom and then stick in position on top of the bodice and resting against the cake. Smooth the join gently to remove ridges, so the bodice trim sits neatly together.

13 To make arms, first split 10g (1/4oz) of skin-tone paste in half. Roll one half into a thin sausage measuring 5cm (2in) in length. Roll one end to round off for the hand and then press down on the hand to flatten slightly. Make a cut on one side for the thumb, cutting down no further than half way and then make three more cuts along the top to separate fingers. Stroke each finger and the thumb to round off and lengthen and then push the thumb down towards the palm to shape the hand.

14 For the elbow, roll the arm gently half way between the wrist and the shoulder to indent slightly and then stick in position. Make the opposite arm in the same way cutting the opposite thumb.

15 Make the fairy's head and nose using the remaining skin-tone modeling paste. Roll a tiny oval-shaped nose and set aside. Roll the remainder into an oval shape and press down to flatten the facial area. Pinch gently either side at the bottom of the face to shape the chin.

16 To make the mouth, roll a tiny sausage of pale pink, press down to flatten and then stick onto her mouth area. Using a knife, cut along the mouth to separate the top and bottom lip. Using a cocktail stick, push up either side of the bottom lip to make it 'v' shaped and then indent into the corners of the mouth to create dimples.

17 For her eyes, roll tiny black oval-shapes for pupils and roll minute eyelashes attaching each using the glue brush. Mark a line under each eye using a knife. Roll tiny eyebrows using pale yellow.

18 To make the wavy skirt effect, roll uneven sausages of differing lengths and shapes using the remaining white and the pale blue and pale pink. Roll out each making them thin but not thin enough to tear and then layer over the skirt securing with edible glue. Trim the top of her bodice with pale pink.

19 Roll different sized uneven sausages using half of the yellow modelling paste and roll flat making the lengths of hair. Twist each carefully to make waves and secure with a little edible glue.

20 With the remaining modelling paste, cut out all the flowers, hearts, stars and dots sticking each in place as soon as they are made. The single petal shaped cutter is used to make the larger flowers with a dot for the centre. To shape the smaller flowers, place them on a foam sheet before indenting with a piping tube (tip) pushed into the centre, making all the petals stand up.

tip

If you prefer, you can paint the facial features with diluted food colouring and a fine paintbrush. Keep the brush quite dry from colour to prevent heavy lines and/or runs. Any painted mistakes can be lifted away using a clean, damp brush.

21 Dust the fairy's cheeks with pink powder colouring and add a little randomly around the dress. Dust the flowers and around the cake board with the yellow powder colouring, deepening the colour around the base of the cake and fading out gently.

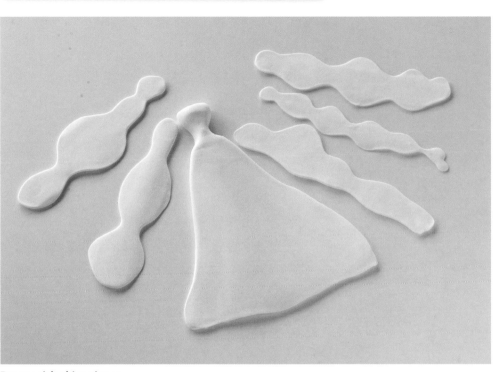

Dress with skirt pieces

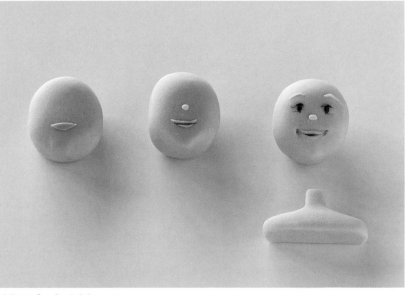

Adding the facial features

The dungeon

What you will need

See pages 7 to 19 for recipes and techniques.

- 2 x 18 cm (7 in) square cakes
- 450 g (1 lb/2c) cake filling
- Icing (powdered) sugar in a sugar shaker

Sugarpaste
- 1.7 kg (3 lb 12 oz) grey
- 30 g (1 oz) black

Modelling paste
- 185 g (6½ oz) grey
- 20 g (¾ oz) black
- 20 g (¾ oz) skin-tone
- 5 g (just under ¼ oz) white

- Edible glue
- Edible silver food colouring

Equipment
- 25 cm (10 in) square cake board
- Large rolling pin
- Cake smoother
- Small plain bladed knife
- Serrated carving knife
- Palette knife
- Ruler
- 2.5 cm (1 in) triangle cutter
- Small scissors
- 9 food-safe paper lolly sticks
- A few cocktail sticks
- No.2 sable paintbrush (for edible glue)

Perfect for the Halloween celebrations, this gruesomely bad creature is locked up tight for the night in his very own dungeon.

Cut out the castellation using a triangle cutter

1 Using a sprinkling of icing (powdered) sugar to prevent sticking, roll out 400 g (14 oz) of grey sugarpaste to a thickness of 2–3 mm (¹⁄₈ in) and use to cover the cake board. Rub the surface with a cake smoother to remove dimples. Trim excess from around the edge and then set aside to dry.

2 Trim the crust from each cake and level the tops. Cut layers in each and then stack one on top of the other. Trim each side of the cake so the sides slope gently inwards making the cake wider around the top. Sandwich all layers together with cake filling assembling on the cake board and then spread a layer over the surface of the cake as a crumb coat and to help the sugarpaste stick.

3 Measure the top of the cake. Roll out 300 g (10½ oz) of grey sugarpaste to a thickness of 3–4 mm (¹⁄₈ in) and use to cover the top of the cake only. Use the cake smoother to smooth along each edge to straighten if necessary. Smooth from the edge inwards to prevent distortion.

4 Make the castellation using 115 g (4 oz) of grey modelling paste edging the top of the cake in four sections covering the two opposite sides first then the back and front. Roll out and

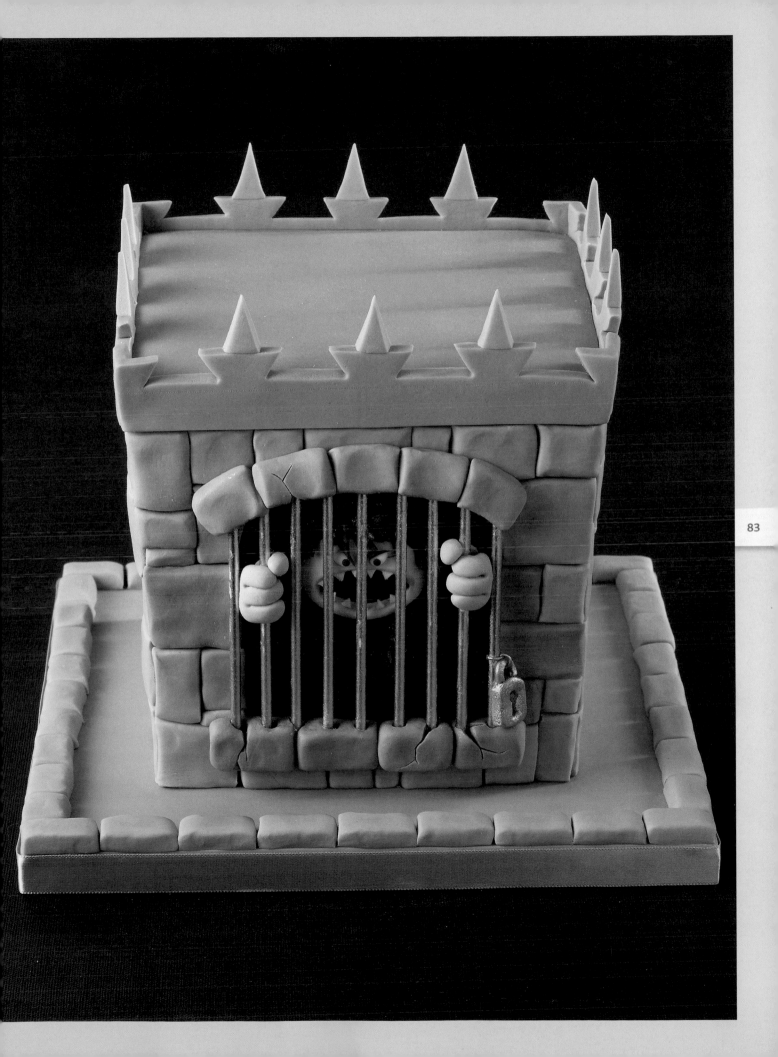

cut strips and then cut out the pattern along the top using the triangle cutter. Cut out long pointed triangles to edge the top of each.

5 Thinly roll out black sugarpaste and cut the shadow area measuring 10 cm (4 in) square and stick in position on the front of the cake. To cover the cake, roll out grey sugarpaste and cut different sized squares and oblong shapes. As each is cut, squeeze along each edge to distort and then stick in position building up little by little until the whole cake surface is covered.

6 Roll out the black modelling paste and snip over the surface with scissors making the fur effect. Tear two patches, one for the fur body and another for the hair.

7 To make the face, roll 10 g (¼ oz) of skin-tone modelling paste into an oval shape and press down to flatten. Cut out the wide mouth area removing the paste and stick the face in position on the front of the cake.

8 Thinly roll out white modelling paste and cut little triangular shaped teeth sticking in position edging the top and bottom of the creature's mouth. Roll two oval shaped eyes and stick on two tiny black circles for pupils. Roll tiny black eyebrows.

9 Make each hand using the remaining skin-tone. The thumbs are separate for ease of sticking around the bars. Roll two teardrop shaped thumbs first and then roll rounded teardrop shapes for the hands pressing down to flatten slightly. Make two cuts to separate three fingers and stroke to round each off at the tip. Curve the hands round gently so each will clasp the bars and be held secure.

tip

For fun, bend the bars so he looks like he's trying to escape.

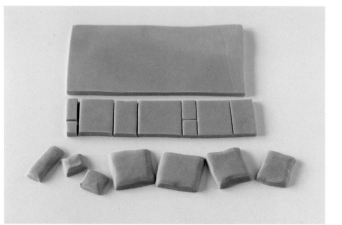

Squeeze the edge at each brick to soften

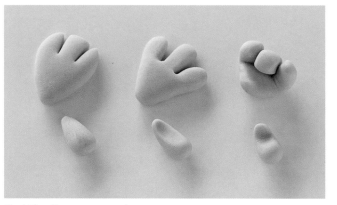

Curl the fingers around

10 To make the bricks that edge along the bottom of the window that hold the bars in place, split 45 g (1½ oz) of grey modelling paste and make four oblong shaped bricks. Stick into position and then supporting the underside of each push a lolly stick along them making holes for the bars. Indent small cracks using a knife.

11 Paint the bars silver and using a little edible glue to secure, stick them upright into the indented holes. To hold the bars in place, model smaller bricks arching across the top using the remaining grey. Stick the hands and thumbs in position wrapped around the bars.

12 Make the lock using the remaining white modelling paste indenting the circle in the centre with the end of a paintbrush and a knife to indent the bottom. Widen the line by moving a damp paintbrush back and forth at the bottom. Stick in position, resting on the brick and against the bar. Roll a small sausage and loop round for the top and make two minute sausages for the links. Paint silver.

13 To complete the dungeon, cut out bricks 2.5 cm (1 in) in length to edge around the cake board pinching each to shape as before (this will make them slightly longer to fit the board).

Head and body shapes

Ragdoll

What you will need

See pages 7 to 19 for recipes and techniques.

- 2 x 15 cm (6 in) square cakes & 2 x 8 cm (3 in) bowl-shaped cakes
- 450 g (1 lb/2c) cake filling
- Icing (powdered) sugar in a sugar shaker

Sugarpaste
- 400 g (14 oz) mid pink
- 770 g (1 lb 11 oz) pale pink
- 115 g (4 oz) white

Modelling paste
- 450 g (1 lb) dark pink
- 115 g (4 oz) white
- 20 g (¾ oz) mid pink
- 85 g (2¾ oz) skin-tone
- 30 g (1 oz) pale brown
- Tiny piece of black

- Edible glue
- Pink powder food colouring

Equipment
- 30 cm (12 in) square cake board
- Large rolling pin
- Cake smoother
- Small plain bladed knife
- Serrated carving knife
- Palette knife
- Two sugar sticks or food-safe internal supports
- A few cocktail sticks
- No.2 sable paintbrush (for edible glue)
- 2.5 cm (1 in) circle cutter
- No.18 PME piping tube (tip) or miniature circle cutter
- Ball tool

Every little girl adores pink. Teaming this with the sweetest ragdoll sitting against a toy box with her bunny rabbit friend makes an exceptionally pretty combination.

Mark the lines for the woodgrain effect

1 Using a sprinkling of icing (powdered) sugar to prevent sticking, roll out the mid pink sugarpaste to a thickness of 2–3 mm (⅛ in) and use to cover the cake board. Rub the surface with a cake smoother to remove any dimples and trim excess from around the edge. Thinly roll out dark pink and cut circles using the circle cutter. Stick over the cake board and smooth gently to inlay into the covering. Set aside to dry.

2 Trim the crust from each cake and level the tops. Cut a layer in each square cake and sandwich all layers together with cake filling making the toy box. Position the cake on the cake board using a dab of cake filling to secure. Sandwich the bowl-shaped cakes together. Spread a layer over the surface of both cakes as a crumb coat and to help the sugarpaste stick and set the spherical cake that will make the ball aside for later.

3 Using the pale pink sugarpaste, roll out to a thickness of 3–4 mm (1/8 in) and cut pieces to cover all sides one at a time covering the two sides first then the back and front. Stick the joins closed with edible glue and rub gently to remove the line. Mark a wood grain pattern over the surface using a knife or a cocktail stick.

4 Roll out and cut a piece to cover the top of the cake and smooth the front edge down to round off making the toy box lid. If required, use a cake smoother to neaten by pressing against the edge. Mark the wood effect as before.

5 To cover the spherical cake, roll out white sugarpaste and cover the cake completely, smoothing down and around the shape stretching out pleats and smoothing excess underneath. Thinly roll out dark pink modelling paste and cut pieces to cover opposite sides of the ball so it seems sectioned into four and smooth the edges into the surface of the covering. Using the piping tube or miniature circle cutter, cut out circles and use for the dotty pattern over the white areas.

6 Split 20 g (¾ oz) of white modelling paste in half and roll two sausage shaped legs. Thinly roll out dark pink and cut out little strips for the stripy pattern.

7 Split 50 g (1¾ oz) of dark pink in half and use to make the shoes. Roll into rounded teardrop shapes and pinch midway to narrow rounding off each toe area. Stick in position using pieces of foam or kitchen paper to support whilst drying.

Shoes and striped socks

8 To make the heels, roll two pea-sized balls of dark pink and press down to flatten. Cut across the top of both and stick in position smoothing gently in place. To make the bow, cut out long, thin strips of white and loop around sticking in place draped over the bottom of each leg and over the shoes.

9 Roll 210 g (7½ oz) of dark pink modelling paste into a teardrop shape and press down to flatten the wide end making the bottom of the dress. Lay the dress down and press at the top to flatten slightly. Thinly roll out white modelling paste and cut circles using the circle cutter. Stick in position along the bottom of the dress twisting

each gently to make a frilled effect. Stick the dress in position over the doll's legs and resting against the toy box for support.

10 Split 15 g (½ oz) in half and roll into long tapering sausages for sleeves. Cut the bottom of each sleeve straight and then stick in position resting either side

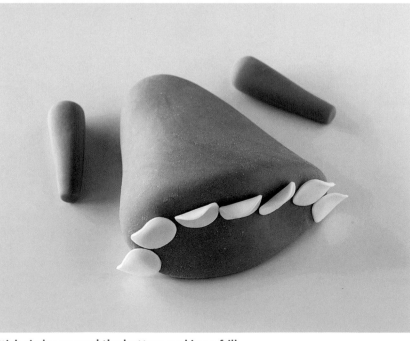

Stick circles around the bottom making a frill

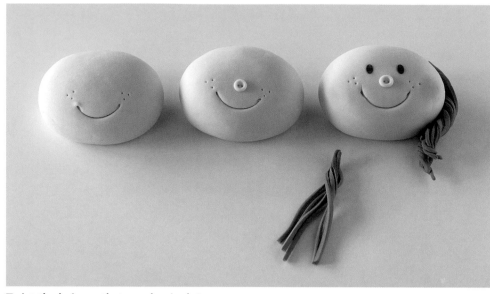

Twist the hair gently to make ringlets

of the Ragdoll's dress and supported by the toy box. Cut out small circles of white using the piping tube and use to make the neck frill.

11 Split 5 g (just under ¼ oz) of skin-tone in half and roll both into teardrop shapes. Press down to flatten slightly and make small cuts either side on each to cut the thumbs, smoothing gently to round off. Cut across the wrist area on both creating a straight edge so they sit neatly against the bottom of each sleeve and stick in place.

12 To make her button nose, roll a tiny ball of skin-tone and press down into the centre using the small end of a ball tool. Indent two tiny holes with a cocktail stick and fill with a minute sausage of pink for the thread.

13 Moisten the area where the head will be with a little edible glue and leave to become tacky. Roll the remaining skin-tone into an oval shape and press down to flatten slightly. Slice a little from the back of the head

making a rough surface; this will stick better against the cake. Indent her smile using the circle cutter pushed in at an upwards angle and indent the corners by pushing in with the end of a paintbrush.

14 Indent freckles using the tip of a cocktail stick. Rub a little pink powder over her cheeks to give her a blush. Roll two tiny black oval shapes for eyes and gently mark across the surface with a knife to give a stitched effect and then stick carefully in position.

15 Roll out and cut strips of brown modelling paste for hair and twist into ringlets. Stick in position framing her face with shorter lengths making her fringe.

16 For the hat brim, roll an oval shape using 35 g (1¼ oz) of dark pink and roll flat using the rolling pin. Stick in position draped over her head with the weight resting on the top of the toy box. Stick a flattened circle of white onto the top for the hat band, using 20g (¾ oz).

Roll 60 g (2 oz) of dark pink into a ball, press to flatten slightly and then stick on top of the hat band to complete the hat.

17 For the rabbit's body, roll a fat teardrop shape using 20 g (¾ oz) of pale pink and stick onto the lap of the Ragdoll's dress. Roll a 10 g (¼ oz) ball for the head pinching to narrow either side slightly. Model a flattened circle for the muzzle and make a tiny cut on the top using a knife.

18 Add a tiny dark pink oval-shaped nose and two tiny black dotted eyes. Push the sugar sticks gently down into the head leaving half protruding ready to help support the ears later.

19 For feet, split 5 g (just under ¼ oz) of pale pink in half and roll into oval shapes. Flatten each and stick in position with a tiny oval shaped mid pink patch. Roll a teardrop shaped patch for his tummy with mid pink, press down and stick in position with the point just under his chin.

20 For arms, split 10 g (¼ oz) of pale pink in half and roll into long teardrop shapes. Do the same for ears using 5 g (just under ¼ oz) but flatten each slightly and stick a teardrop shaped patch of mid pink onto the centre. To make holes in the ears for the sugar sticks, push a cocktail stick into the bottom of each and then remove. Push each ear down onto the sugar stick securing at the bottom with a little edible glue.

21 To make the small stripy ball, separately roll a white and dark pink ball using 50 g (1¾ oz) for each and then cut into quarters keeping the cuts as precise as possible. Stick alternate quarters together using a little edible glue and then gently roll the resulting ball in your hands to close the joins, taking care any excess doesn't distort the shape. Roll some of the remaining white and pink together until marbled and use for the small ball on top of the toy box.

tip
If the rabbit's ears need support whilst drying, roll up kitchen paper and wedge it carefully between the ears and the cake board surface. Gently remove when dry.

Troll house

What you will need

See pages 7 to 19 for recipes and techniques.

- 20 cm (8 in) square cake
- 450 g (1 lb/2 c) cake filling
- Icing (powdered) sugar in a sugar shaker

Sugarpaste
- 625 g (1 lb 6 oz) brown
- 900 g (2 lb) stone (cream with a touch of black)
- 30 g (1 oz) black
- 400 g (14 oz) cream
- 60 g (2 oz) green

Modelling paste
- 20 g (¾ oz) skin tone
- 10 g (¼ oz) orange
- 30 g (1 oz) cream
- 30 g (1 oz) dark cream
- 30 g (1 oz) pale grey
- 30 g (1 oz) grey
- Small piece of white
- Small piece of dark pink

- Edible glue

Equipment
- 30 cm (12 in) round cake board
- Large rolling pin
- Small plain bladed knife
- Serrated carving knife
- Palette knife
- A few cocktail sticks
- 4 cm (1¾ in) circle cutter
- 30 cm (12 in) ruler
- No.2 sable paintbrush (for edible glue)
- Kitchen paper
- Large star piping tube (tip) or kitchen fork

This naughty troll needs a lesson in good manners, but he's only trying to ward off all the candle blowers to leave his house alone!

Push the covering inwards towards the base

1 Knead 400 g (14 oz) of brown sugarpaste until soft and pliable. Using a sprinkling of icing (powdered) sugar to prevent sticking, roll out and use to cover the cake board. Cut wavy lines around the edge exposing some cake board for the grass later and then set aside to dry.

2 Trim the crust from the cake and slice the top flat. Cut the cake exactly in half and cut a layer in each. Place all layers one on top of the other. Cut 2.5 cm (1 in) from one end making a cake measuring 18 x 10 cm (7 x 4 in) and then sandwich all layers together with cake filling. Spread a layer over the surface of the cake as a crumb coat and to help the sugarpaste stick. Position the cake on the cake board.

3 Roll out the stone coloured sugarpaste and cover the cake completely, stretching out pleats and smoothing downwards. Trim excess from around the base. Press with your hands to indent the surface.

4 Cut the front and side windows next using the circle cutter. Use the top of the circle cutter only for the large front window and then to gain the shape, cut down either side and along the bottom using a knife. Cut the large crack on the front of the house and indent more cracks around it and around the house.

5 Fill windows with thinly rolled out black sugarpaste, fill the crack with thinly rolled out sausages of brown for a wood effect and then add window bars to the round window. Roll an uneven sausage of brown and use for the windowsill.

6 Roll out the cream sugarpaste and cut an oblong to cover either side of the roof. Indent lines across the surface using a ruler. Stick in position with a little edible glue and then make small cuts around the edge using a knife. Cut horizontal lines flicking up excess slightly.

7 Using 90 g (3 oz) of brown sugarpaste, roll into a fat sausage and make cuts to separate branches. Twist each branch gently to stretch and roll to thin out at the tip. Mark the wood effect by stroking the surface repeatedly with the end of

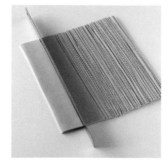

Texture the roof using a ruler

the paintbrush. Stick into position using strips of rolled up kitchen paper to support whilst drying. Add more branches and blend in the join by smoothing gently with a little edible glue.

8 Model different sized 'stones' for the chimney using the cream, dark cream, pale grey and grey modelling paste, pinching each to gain an angular shape and then build up against the side of the house graduating in size. Finish with a small ring of pale grey for the chimney top. Stick a few flattened stones next to the front window and edge the round window.

9 To make the Troll's face and cheeks, split 15 g (just under ¼ oz) of the skin-tone modelling paste in half, roll one half into an oval-shape and press down to flatten slightly. Indent at one end to shape the top of his head. To make his cheeks, roll the second half into a fat sausage and roll gently in the centre to narrow. Stroke down along the bottom edge to shape his chin. Stick this piece onto his face and then cut his mouth, deepening the cut slightly on one side. For his nose, roll a small ball into a teardrop shape and indent nostrils using the end of a paintbrush. Stick two flattened white circles either side for his eyes with two black pupils.

10 Moisten the window area with glue and leave to become tacky. Cut a slice off the back of the Troll's head to flatten and make a slightly rough surface; this will help the head stick firmly into the window. For his ears, take one third of the remaining skin-tone and split in half. Roll into oval shapes and indent into

Twist out the branches to lengthen

the centre of each using your fingertip. Stick in position bending each forward.

11 Split the remaining skin-tone in half and use to make the Troll's hands. To make a hand, roll a teardrop and press down to flatten slightly. Make a cut on one side for the thumb and then two more cuts along the top to separate three fingers. Round off each fingertip by pinching gently. Bend the hand round and stick in position wrapped around an ear. Repeat for the second hand cutting an opposite thumb.

12 Make all the hair pieces using the orange modelling paste, sticking around the top of the Troll's head. Model his two tiny orange eyebrows. For his tongue, roll the dark pink into a teardrop shape and indent a line at the narrow end. Stick into the Troll's mouth.

13 To make the grass, roll out the green sugarpaste and texture heavily by cutting the surface repeatedly with the star piping tube, or use a kitchen fork. Tear gently apart and stick in clumps over the cake board.

Shapes to build up the troll

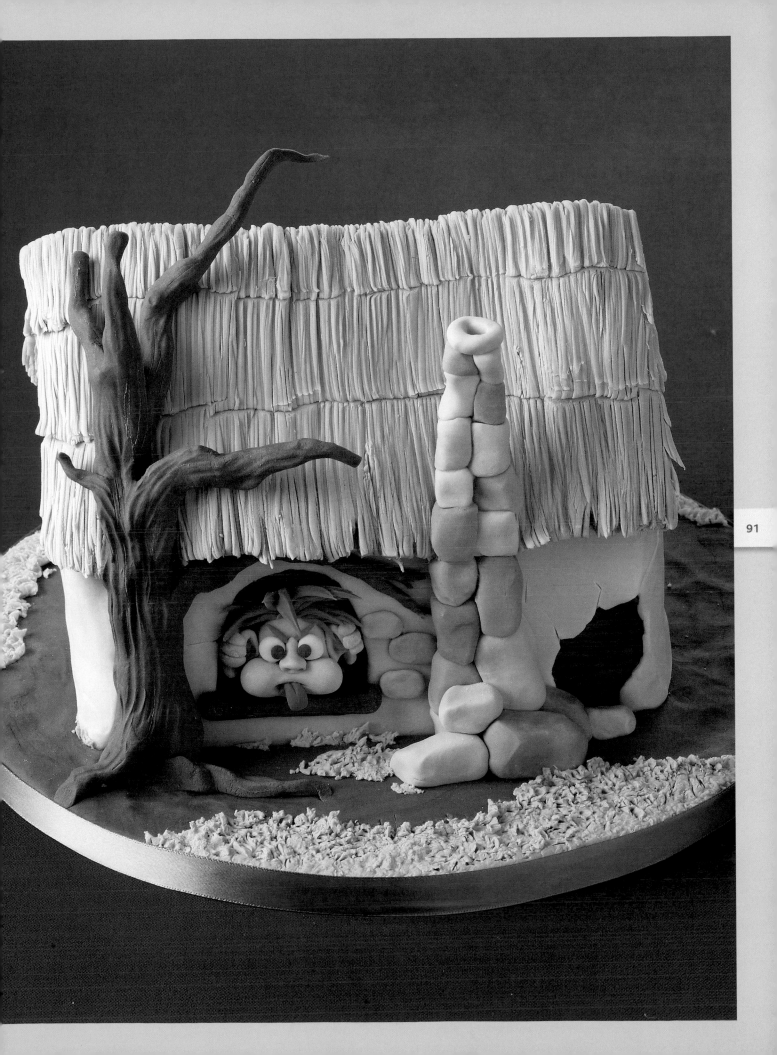

Glass slipper

What you will need

See pages 7 to 19 for recipes and techniques.

- 25 cm (10 in) round cake
- 450 g (1 lb/2 c) cake filling
- Icing (powdered) sugar in a sugar shaker

Sugarpaste
- 450 g (1 lb) pale blue
- 1.25 kg (2 lb 12 oz) mid blue

Modelling paste
- 210 g (7 ½ oz) white
- 145 g (5 oz) mid blue

- Edible glue
- Edible or food-safe silver colouring
- Edible or food-safe silver glitter

Equipment
- 35 cm (14 in) round cake board
- Large rolling pin
- Small plain bladed knife
- Serrated carving knife
- Palette knife
- Cake smoother
- Templates (see page 126)
- Kitchen paper
- A few cocktail sticks
- No.2 sable paintbrush (for edible glue)
- Miniature star cutter

Every little girl dreams of fitting into Cinderella's glass slipper and here it is twinkling with silver sparkle, a child size that can be kept as a memento of the lucky girl's special day.

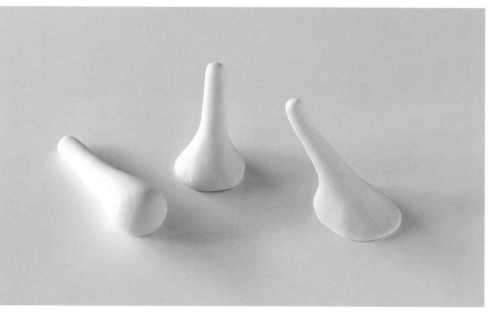

Heel shape

tip

If short of time, make the sole of the slipper out of a cake card, covering the top with a thin layer of modelling paste and then bend into shape.

1 Using a sprinkling of icing (powdered) sugar to prevent sticking, roll out the pale blue sugarpaste to a thickness of 2–3 mm (¹/₈ in) and use to cover the cake board. Smooth the surface with a cake smoother and then trim excess from around the edge. To remove excess icing (powdered) sugar, rub the surface with a snall ball of sugarpaste. Set aside to dry.

2 Make the slipper next to allow for drying time. Make the heel first using 30 g (1 oz) of white modelling paste. Roll into a long rounded teardrop shape and flatten the full end by pressing down onto the work surface. Flatten the bottom of the heel or cut straight. Bend into shape so the heel falls forwards slightly and then set aside to dry upturned on the full end.

3 Using the template, roll out and cut the sole shape using 45 g (1½ oz) of white modelling paste. Smooth around the outside edge to round off and then bend in position resting on rolled up kitchen paper. Check that the heel sits well underneath and adjust if necessary and then stick into position.

4 Cut out the top of the slipper and bend into shape. Moisten around the outside edge of the sole at the front with a little edible glue and leave to become tacky. To help keep the front of the shoe in shape, roll a ball of modelling paste using 45 g (1½ oz), flatten slightly and dust with icing (powdered) sugar to prevent sticking. Place down onto the front of the shoe and then stick the top of the slipper in position.

5 For the back of the slipper, roll out and cut the shape from the template and stick in position smoothing the top edge over slightly.

6 Trim the crust from the cake and level the top. Trim off the top edge to round off cutting down to mid-

way. Turn the cake over and repeat. Trim a little out of the centre for the dip in which the button will sit. Cut two layers in the cake and sandwich together with cake filling. Spread a layer over the surface of the cake as a crumb coat and to help the sugarpaste stick and position on the cake board.

7 Roll out the mid blue sugarpaste and cover the cake completely, smoothing down and around the shape. Cut a neat edge leaving around 5 cm (2 in) excess and then tuck this underneath, smoothing carefully in place.

8 Indent a channel around the edge of the cake ready for the rope and moisten along this indentation with edible glue. Make the rope in four sections spaced evenly around the cake with the joins hidden with tassels. To make a rope section, split 10 g (¼ oz) in half and roll two sausages 20 cm (8 in) in length. Moisten along one rope with a little edible glue and then stick one on top of the other. Twist from the centre out to opposite ends and then stick the resulting

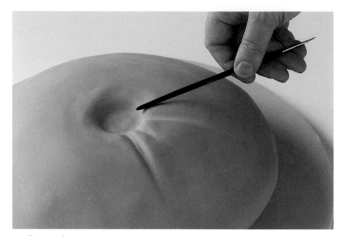

Making pleats

Twist gently for rope effect

twisted rope in place on the cake. Repeat until four sections are complete.

9 Split 45 g (1½ oz) of mid blue modelling paste into four pieces and roll into teardrop shapes. Press each flat and cut repeatedly into the surface to indent lines for tassels. Stick in place with a small ball for the tie indented in the centre with the end of a paintbrush. Stick a small, flattened ball onto the centre of the cake making the button.

10 With the remaining mid blue modelling paste, roll a thin sausage that will support the line of stars from the top of the cushion. Roll to a length of 20 cm (8 in). Stick this onto the cushion draping

down onto the cake board. Cut out 120 stars using the miniature star cutter and paint them with the silver colouring. Stick them over the cushion and cake board followed with a sprinkling of silver glitter.

11 Position the slipper onto the centre of the cake and secure with a little edible glue. Paint the slipper with the silver colouring and sprinkle with silver glitter.

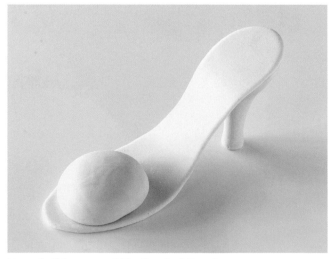

Use a ball to support the front of the shoe

Hey monster!

What you will need

See pages 7 to 19 for recipes and techniques.

- 2 x 15 cm (6 in) round cakes & 1 x 15 cm (6 in) dia. bowl-shaped cake
- 625 g (1 lb 6 oz/2¾ c) cake filling
- Icing (powdered) sugar in a sugar shaker

Sugarpaste
- 450 g (1 lb) grey
- 2kg (4lb 7oz) purple
- 25g (just over ¾ oz) white
- Tiny piece of black

- Edible glue

Equipment
- 30 cm (12 in) round cake board
- Large rolling pin
- Small plain bladed knife
- Serrated carving knife
- Palette knife
- New plastic pan scourer or food-safe texture mat
- Bone or ball tool (optional)

- A few cocktail sticks
- No.2 sable paintbrush (for edible glue)

This fun character certainly grabs your attention with his gruesome looks but gorgeous expression. He's easy to make too, so you should complete him in a relatively short time.

1 Using a sprinkling of icing (powdered) sugar to prevent sticking, roll out the grey sugarpaste to a thickness of 2–3mm (⅛ in) and use to cover the cake board. Press the rolling pin over the surface to create ripples and then trim excess from around the edge. Using trimmings, model small oval shaped pebbles and stick them over the cake board. Put aside to dry.

2 Trim the crust from each cake and level the tops. Cut a layer in each and then using cake filling, sandwich all cakes together with the bowl-shaped cake on the top. At this stage the cake should be at least 20 cm (8 in) in height. Spread a layer over the surface of the cake to use as a crumb coat and help the sugarpaste stick. Position the cake on the cake board slightly towards the back.

Pad out the shape before covering

tip

If you prefer, replace the leg padding with two cupcakes

3 Pad out the legs next by splitting 200 g (7 oz) of purple sugarpaste in half, rolling into balls and then smoothing each against the base of the cake leaving a small space in between. For his tummy, roll 60 g (2 oz) into a ball and press flat, smoothing around the edge to thin out and then stick onto the front smoothing the edge in line with the surface of the cake, leaving a space between the tummy and legs.

Smooth the top lip and then texture

4 Roll out 1 kg (2 lb 3¼ oz) of purple sugarpaste and texture the surface using the plastic scourer or texture mat. Carefully roll up opposite sides and then place against the front of the cake. Unroll the covering around the sides and trim away any excess. Secure the join closed at the back with a little edible glue and texture the surface to disguise the join.

5 Split 75 g (2½ oz) of purple sugarpaste in half. For the top lip, roll one half into a fat sausage and smooth along the top edge to thin out. Stick in position using a little edible glue and texture the join to remove completely. Mark creases using the paintbrush handle. For the bottom lip, roll the remaining piece into an uneven sausage rounding off each end and then stick in position using a bone or ball tool or your fingertip to indent each end. Mark creases as before.

6 For his nose, roll 35 g (1¼ oz) of purple sugarpaste into a teardrop shape and indent each nostril. Pinch either side to indent and then stick in position resting on his top lip. Stick three tiny balls over his nose for his warts.

7 Model three small teardrop shaped white teeth and stick in position curling slightly inwards. Split the remaining white in half and use for eyes and then stick on two black pupils. For eyebrows, split 30g (1oz) of purple in half and roll into long teardrop shapes. Stick in position smoothing the narrower end into the surface of the cake and texturing to hide the join as before.

8 For his ears, split 10 g (¼ oz) of purple sugarpaste in half. Roll into fat sausage shapes and then pinch to round off each end. Indent into the centres using your fingertip and then put each aside for a few moments to firm up before sticking in position and smoothing the joins closed as before.

9 To make his hands, split 175 g (6 oz) of purple sugarpaste in half. Roll one half into a rounded teardrop shape and press down to flatten slightly. Make a cut for the thumb on one side, cutting down no further than halfway in length. Make two more cuts along the top to separate fingers and then round each off by pinching gently. Push the thumb down towards the palm and then

tip

If you'd prefer him a bit more fierce looking, lower each eyebrow down over his eyes so he glowers at you.

curl the fingers round. Make the second hand cutting the opposite thumb.

10 Split 225 g (8 oz) of purple in half and roll into sausages 14 cm (5½ in) in length and texture as before. Stick in position with a hand turned out at the bottom of each. Stick small teardrop shapes around the bottom of each arm for longer fur and then make some extra for the bottom of each ear.

11 For his feet, split 185 g (6½ oz) of purple in half, roll into ball shapes and stick in position at the bottom of each leg, texturing as before. Make his toes with the purple trimmings, each with flattened circles for toenails.

97

Indent one large and one small nostril

Curve the hand by gently pressing into the palm

Midnight fairies

What you will need

See pages 7 to 19 for recipes and techniques.

- 20 cm (8 in) & 10 cm (4 in) round cakes
- 450 g (1 lb/2 c) cake filling
- Icing (powdered) sugar in a sugar shaker

Sugarpaste
- 1 kg (2 lb 3¼ oz) blue

Modelling paste
- 450g (1lb) palest blue
- 450g (1lb) dark blue
- 20g (¾ oz) skin-tone
- 20g (¾ oz) pale yellow
- Tiny piece of black

- Edible glue
- Edible sparkle powder

Equipment
- 25 cm (10 in) round cake board
- Large rolling pin
- Small plain bladed knife
- Serrated carving knife
- Palette knife
- No's 1, 3, 4, 16 & 18 (PME) piping tubes (tips)
- A few cocktail sticks
- No.2 sable paintbrush (for edible glue)
- 4 x 20 cm (8 in) plastic dowelling
- Blossom plunger cutter
- Flower cutter
- 3 x sugar sticks or food-safe internal support
- Small pieces of food-safe foam sponge or kitchen paper

I initially intended to make a daytime scene, with green covered cakes and red and white spotted toadstools with fairies in bright fun colours. But then I imagined them at midnight, when moonlight turns everything that magical shade of blue.

Making the fairy wings

1 To allow for plenty of drying time, make the fairy wings first using 5g (just under ¼ oz) of pale blue modelling paste for each pair. To make a wing, roll into a sausage that tapers at both ends and roll out the shape using a rolling pin. Cut out different sized circles from the surface to make a lacy effect and then set aside to dry.

2 Trim the crust from each cake and level the tops. Cut a layer in each and assemble on the cake board with the larger cake slightly off centre and the smaller cake positioned towards the back for a stepped effect. Sandwich all the layers with cake filling. Spread a layer over the surface of the cake as a crumb coat and to help the sugarpaste stick.

3 Using a sprinkling of icing (powdered) sugar to prevent sticking, roll out the blue sugarpaste to a thickness of 3–4 mm (⅛ in) and use to cover the cake and cake board completely. Smooth around the shape pinching gently along the top edges and smoothing ridges over the surface. Trim excess from around the edge.

4 There are six toadstools, which need a support inside to help hold their weight. To make the stalk of the tallest, roll 30 g (1 oz) of palest blue modelling paste into an uneven sausage narrower in the centre and insert a dowel down through the middle leaving a little protruding at the top with the remainder at the bottom which will be inserted into the cake.

5 Cut the top and bottom of the stalk straight; it should now measure around 10 cm (4 in). Make the stalks for the remaining toadstools using between 25 g (just over ¾ oz) and 10 g (¼ oz) for each, inserting a dowel down through all except for the one at the front, which is supported by the side of the cake. You will need to cut the dowels for the shorter stalks, do this by scoring and then snapping to break.

6 For the pleated underside of the largest toadstool, roll 50 g (1¾ oz) of pale blue into a ball and press down to flatten into a dome shape. Mark pleats using the back of a knife and then stick onto the top of the stalk using a little edible glue. Repeat for the smaller different sized stalks using between 40 g (1½ oz) and 20 g (¾ oz) for each.

7 To make the top of each toadstool, set 10 g (¼ oz) of dark blue aside for later and then split the remainder into seven pieces, all slightly different in size with the largest weighing 115 g (4 oz). Roll each into a ball and press down to flatten around the outside edge making a dome shape and then stick in place onto the top of the toadstool.

8 Repeat for all the toadstools and then push each into the cake starting with the smallest at the front and stick them together where they touch using a little edible glue. Add misshapen different sized flattened dots to the top of each smoothing in line with the surface.

9 To make their legs, split 10 g (¼ oz) of skin-tone into six equally sized pieces. To make a leg, roll one into a sausage shape 4 cm (1½ in) in length. Pinch out one end bending the top over to make the foot. Squeeze to lengthen and pinch to indent the arch on the underside.

tip

To remove any excess icing (powdered) sugar, rub gently over the surface with a small ball of sugarpaste. This will lift away any remaining residue and leave a clean, smooth surface.

10 Place the leg down on the work surface and pinch up the knee half-way between the ankle and the top of the leg. Push in behind the knee to shape the leg. Bend into its pose and as each is made stick in place with a little edible glue.

11 Split 5 g (just under ¼ oz) of pale blue into three pieces, roll into ball shapes and then stick over the top of each pair of legs. For the bodice, split 10 g (¼ oz) into three and model teardrop shapes. Press down onto the centre to flatten the stomach pushing up the excess for the chest area and stick in position with a sugar stick inserted down through each

to help hold it in place, leaving a little protruding at the top to hold the heads in position later.

12 For the skirt, roll out and cut different lengths of pale blue and indent pleats over the surface of each using the paintbrush handle. Stick in position draped over the fairy's laps.

13 Split 5 g (just under ¼ oz) of skin-tone into six pieces. To make an arm, roll one into a sausage measuring 2.5 cm (1 in) in length. Roll gently at one end to indent the wrist and round off the hand. Press down on the hand to flatten slightly and then make a cut halfway for the

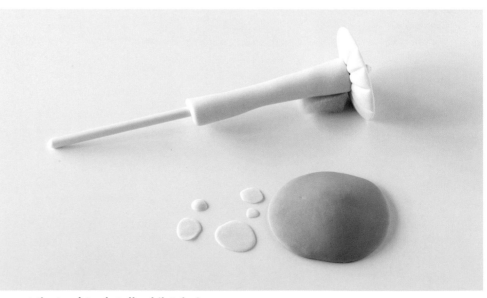

Support the toadstool stalk whilst drying

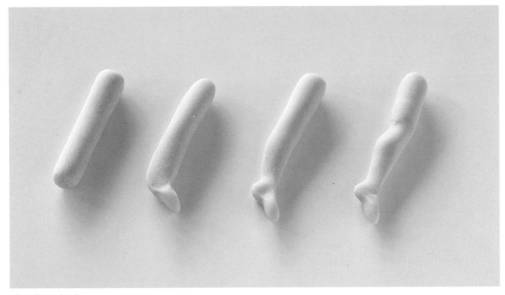

Shaping the legs

thumb on one side. Make three further cuts along the top to separate fingers and then stroke each gently to round off and lengthen. Push the thumb down towards the palm to shape the hand.

14 To indent the elbows, roll gently halfway between the wrist and the shoulder and then stick the arm in position holding for a few moments until secure.

15 Roll out the black modelling paste as thinly as possible and set aside to firm up but not dry. To make their heads, first roll minute ball noses and then split the remainder into three and roll their ball shaped heads. Press down to flatten each face slightly and then indent their smiles by pushing in the tip of the no.16 piping tube at an upwards angle. Dimple the corners using a cocktail stick.

16 Cut out their eyes from the rolled out black using the no.1 piping tube. Roll different sized lengths of pale yellow and layer over their heads building up the long

flowing hair. Stick the wings in position using small pieces of foam sponge or rolled up kitchen paper to support whilst drying.

17 Using the modelling paste trimmings, roll out and cut all the flowers and model tiny pebbles for the cake surface. For the dark

blue pulled flowers, roll tiny teardrop shapes and press the full end down onto the end of the paintbrush. Make even cuts around the edge, remove the paintbrush and then pinch out petals. Sprinkle the flowers and top of each toadstool with edible sparkle powder.

tip

If short of time, pipe the hair with pale yellow royal icing, building up piped layers from a piping bag with a small hole cut into the tip. Use a damp paintbrush to flick out tendrils around the face.

101

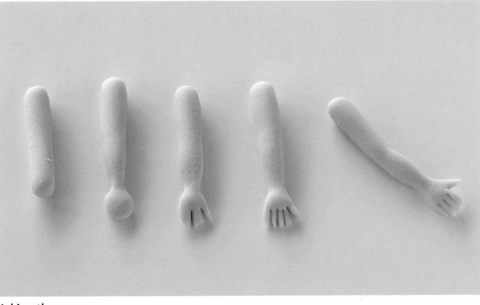

Making the arms

Ugly bug

What you will need

See pages 7 to 19 for recipes and techniques.

- 2 x 15 cm (6 in) dia. bowl-shaped cakes
- 450 g (1 lb/2 c) cake filling
- Icing (powdered) sugar in a sugar shaker
- Edible glue

Sugarpaste
- 400 g (14 oz) yellow
- 900 g (2 lb) lime green

Modelling Paste
- 685 g (1 lb 8 oz) lime green
- 45 g (1½ oz) yellow
- 60 g (2 oz) orange
- 30 g (1 oz) black

Equipment
- 30 cm (12 in) round cake board
- Large rolling pin
- Small plain bladed knife
- Serrated carving knife
- Palette knife
- 1 x food safe plastic dowelling
- No.2 sable paintbrush (for edible glue)
- Kitchen paper (for support)

A rather gruesome bug, but with his happy appealing face he may not be quite as unwelcome. One thing's for sure he will certainly taste better than the real thing.

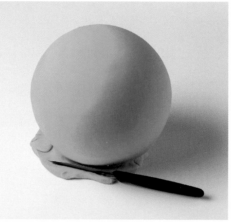

Trim excess from around the base

Insert a dowel to support the head

Cake Board

1 Using the yellow sugarpaste, roll out and cover the cake board (see page 18, how to cover a cake board) and then set aside to dry.

Cake

2 Trim the crust from each cake, level the tops and then cut a layer in each cake near the top so all the layers are central when assembled to help stabilise the cake. Sandwich all layers together with cake filling

and then spread a layer over the surface of the cake as a crumb coat to seal the cake and help the sugarpaste stick.

3 Roll out 900 g (2 lb) of lime green sugarpaste to a thickness of 3–4mm (1/8 in) and cover the cake completely, gently smoothing downwards to expel trapped air and stretching out pleats around the base. Trim away excess and use a palette knife to smooth around the bottom. Position the cake on the cake board. To remove dimples and gain a smooth surface, roll a small

ball of sugarpaste and rub against the surface as a cake smoother.

4 Roll three graduating ball shapes for the end of his body using 240 g (8½ oz) of lime green modelling paste, flattening each slightly and sticking in position curling around. For his chest, split 160 g (5½ oz) in half and roll two oval shapes. Press down hard on one flattening it and then press lighter on the second so the shape is thicker. Stick these in position and then roll a 45 g (1½ oz) ball

Head and face shapes

Back view

of lime green and stick onto the centre for his neck. Push the doweling down through them all and into the cake ready to support his head.

Head

5 Roll a teardrop shaped head using 170 g (5¾ oz) of lime green modelling paste. Push down onto the dowel to make a hole and then remove and allow to dry so the weight will be held by the dowel and not the cake. Using the step picture as a guide, model the facial features with the remaining lime green modelling paste adding large orange oval-shaped eyes using 15 g (½ oz) for each.

6 To make his tongue, model a small ball of orange and indent down the centre using the back of a knife. Stick in position resting on the bottom lip. Stick a yellow nose onto his face and then using the remainder shape different sized sausage shapes and press flat to make the tummy scales. When his head is dry, stick in position supported by the dowel.

7 Using the remaining orange, roll out and cut the different sized patches for his back, smoothing them in line with the cake surface. Add a small ball to the end of his tail.

8 To make his legs, split 10 g (¼ oz) of black modelling paste into four pieces and model long tapering sausage shapes. Stick each in position with the full end uppermost. For feet, split 10 g (¼ oz) into four and model teardrop shapes. Press down on each to flatten and then cut twice in each, turning out each point. Stick in position on the cake board with the end of the legs resting on top.

9 Using the remaining black modelling paste make his two pupils, the curled antenna and two wings. The antenna and wings are flattened tapering sausage shapes curled around into a spiral. Leave the wings to firm before positioning, and then use rolled up kitchen paper to support their shape whilst drying.

Making a foot

Fairy wand

What you will need

See pages 7 to 19 for recipes and techniques.

- 1 x 30 cm (12 in) square cake
- 450 g (1 lb/2 c) cake filling
- Icing (powdered) sugar in a sugar shaker

Sugarpaste
- 450 g (1 lb) white
- 900 g (2 lb) pale pink

Modelling paste
- 95 g (3¼ oz) white
- 30 g (1 oz) pale pink
- 30 g (1 oz) red
- 35 g (1¼ oz) skin tone
- Tiny piece of black
- 30 g (1 oz) pale yellow

Royal icing
- 5 g (just under ¼ oz) white

- Edible glue
- Sugar stick or food-safe internal support
- Edible silver colouring
- Edible silver glitter or sparkle powder
- Pink powder colouring

Equipment
- 35 cm (14 in) square thick cake card
- 12 cm (5 in) round or square thick cake card (optional)
- Template (see page 127)
- Large scissors
- Large rolling pin
- Small plain bladed knife
- Serrated carving knife
- Palette knife
- Cake smoother
- A few cocktail sticks
- No.2 sable paintbrush (for edible glue)
- Clear plastic food-safe dowel
- 0.6 m (2 ft) length of red/white dot ribbon
- 1.3 m (4 ft 2 in) length of white/red dot ribbon
- 1 cm (¼ in) circle cutter
- Ball tool (optional)
- No.16 (PME) piping tube (tip)
- Foam pieces or kitchen paper (for support)

Every little girl would love this cute funky fairy sitting on a cake shaped into a magical fairy wand.

Use the template to make the star shape

1 Using the template (see page 127) cut out the star shape from the 35 cm (14 in) square cake card. With a sprinkling of icing (powdered) sugar to prevent sticking, roll out the white sugarpaste to a thickness of 2-3mm (1/8 in)and use to cover the star-shaped cake card. Smooth the surface with a cake smoother and then trim around the shape. Apply the silver colouring to the outside edge of the board and then set aside to dry.

tip

Stick the smaller cake card centrally underneath the star shaped cake board. This will prevent the possibility of the weight of the cake distorting the board causing damage to the cake.

2 Trim the crust from the cake and level the top. Using the cake template cut out the star shape using some of the trimmings to gain the two opposite longer points. Cut a layer in the cake and then sandwich with filling. Position the cake on the cake board and then spread a layer over the surface of the cake as a crumb coat to seal the cake and help the sugarpaste stick.

3 Roll out the pink sugarpaste and use to cover the cake completely. Smooth around the shape using the cake smoother to help flatten the sides of each point. Trim excess from around the edge. Rub the top surface with a cake smoother to remove any dimples.

4 Tie the red/white dot ribbon to one end of the dowel and twist around, tying a large bow at the end. Gently push the wand into the sugarpaste covering at the bottom of a long star point and then remove. Set aside for later.

5 Make the wings first to allow for drying time. Split 15 g (just under ¾ oz) of white modelling paste in half and roll each into long thin sausage shapes measuring 35 cm (14 in) in length. Using a little edible glue to secure, roll up each end one larger than the other and then set aside to dry.

6 To make the legs, split 10 g (¼ oz) of pink modelling paste in half and roll two long thin sausages. Thinly roll out red and cut tiny strips, sticking each in place with a little edible glue. To make her shoes, split 5 g (just under ¼ oz) of red in half. Roll one half into a rounded teardrop shape and indent a heel on the base at the narrow end using the flat of a knife. Make another shoe and stick each in position with a small strip of white for stocks indented with the back of a knife.

7 To make her dress, roll 75 g (2½ oz) of white modelling paste into a ball and then roll back and forth slightly off centre to indent her waist, rounding off each end one larger than the other. Press down to flatten the larger end and smooth around the edge making her skirt. Lay the dress down and press slightly at the opposite end and then cut straight across using a knife. Stick her dress in position on top of her legs ensuring the figure is sitting upright. Thinly roll out pink and cut three strips to decorate her dress.

8 Roll a fat sausage using 5 g (just under ¼ oz) of skin-tone modelling paste and pinch halfway to make the neck. Stick in position and then push the food-safe internal support down through the neck and into the dress, leaving some protruding to support the head later.

tip

As an alternative to the plastic wand, you could replace with a thin stick of striped rock candy.

Dress shape

Making the cute expression

9 Moisten either side of the body with edible glue and leave to become tacky. Split 5 g (just under ¼ oz) of skin-tone in half. To make an arm, roll one half into a sausage shape and pinch gently to round off one end for the hand. Press the hand down to flatten slightly. Cut a thumb first cutting down halfway. Make three more straight and slightly shorter cuts along the top to separate fingers. Stroke each gently to lengthen and round off.

10 Push the thumb down towards the palm and bend the fingers around together gently. Make the second arm cutting the opposite thumb and stick both arms in position holding for a few moments until secure.

11 Thinly roll out the remaining pink and cut a strip for the collar, wrapping it gently around her shoulders to hide the join. Thinly roll out red and cut two small buttons a small square pocket decorating it with circles of pale pink, made by rolling tiny balls and pressing flat or use the piping tube for larger dots.

12 Set aside a tiny piece of skin-tone for her nose later and then roll the remainder into a ball for her head. Indent her smile by pushing the circle cutter in at an upwards angle and dimple each corner using a cocktail stick. To make her nose, roll a tiny ball and stick onto her face indenting nostrils using the end of a paintbrush.

13 Indent two eye sockets using the small end of a ball tool or use the end of a paintbrush and roll gently round. Roll two tiny white eyes and two smaller black pupils.

14 For eyelashes, break off a minute amount of black using a cocktail stick. Roll this minute piece into a sausage making an eyelash and drop onto the work surface. To apply, moisten the eye area with a little glue, wipe the excess glue from the brush making it only slightly sticky and then pick up the eyelash with the brush using this to apply the eyelash. Repeat for the opposite eye and make two eyelashes on each. Take care not to move over the black causing it to smudge.

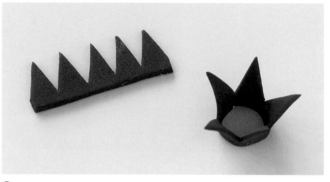

Crown

15 Dust a little pink powder over her cheeks to give her a blush. To make the crown, thinly roll out the remaining red modelling paste and cut a strip measuring 2 x 5 cm (¾ x 2 in). Cut out triangles along the top and then loop round securing the join closed. Stick in position on top of her head. Roll different sized spirals of pale yellow paste to make the hair.

16 The wings are quite heavy so when dry secure with a dab of the royal icing using pieces of food-safe foam sponge or small strips of rolled up kitchen paper to hold in position until secure. Sprinkle edible glitter or sparkle around the edge of the cake. Stick the wand handle in position.

tip

If short of time, pipe the hair with pale yellow royal icing. Pipe spirals over her head with smaller spirals around her face using a piping bag with a small hole cut into the tip.

Worms

What you will need

See pages 7 to 19 for recipes and techniques.

- 1 x 20 cm (8 in) & 1 x 10 cm (4 in) round cakes
- 450 g (1 lb/2 c) cake filling
- Icing (powdered) sugar in a sugar shaker

Sugarpaste
- 625 g (1 lb 6 oz) pale brown
- 665 g (1 lb 7½ oz) bright green

Modelling paste
- 285 g (10 oz) pale pink
- 5 g (just under ¼ oz) white
- 10 g (¼ oz) black
- 45 g (1 ½ oz) cream
- 10 g (¼ oz) pale green

- Edible glue

Equipment
- 30 cm (12 in) round cake board
- Large rolling pin
- Small plain bladed knife
- Serrated carving knife
- Palette knife
- Ruler
- A few cocktail sticks
- No.2 sable paintbrush (for edible glue)
- Large star piping tube (for texture)
- Paper lolly stick or food-safe plastic dowelling
- 2.5 cm (1 in) circle cutter
- Kitchen paper (for support)

Many children would love to keep worms as pets, but this fun design could be a gentle reminder that worms prefer to live in the garden and not in little boy's pockets!

Unroll covering around the cake sides

1 Trim the crust from each cake and level the tops. Cut a layer in each and then sandwich all layers together with the smaller cake on top, positioned slightly towards the back. Position both cakes onto the cake board slightly towards the back for a staggered effect, securing with a little cake filling. Spread a layer of cake filling over the surface of both cakes as a crumb coat and to help the sugarpaste stick.

2 Knead 400 g (14 oz) of pale brown sugarpaste until soft and pliable. Using a little icing (powdered) sugar to prevent sticking, roll out and cut a strip measuring 60 cm (24 in) and the depth measurement of the bottom cake. Indent uneven vertical lines over the surface using the rolling pin and then roll into a spiral so it's easy to lift. Position against the cake and unroll the covering around it, trimming away excess and

Texturing the grass

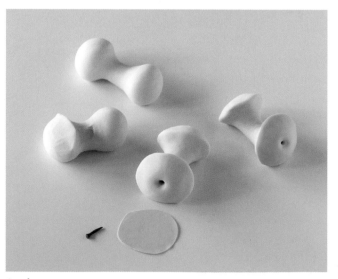

Making the cute expression

securing the join closed with a little edible glue. Rub the join closed with your fingers to remove completely. Repeat for the smaller cake using the remaining pale brown, cutting the strip to a length of 35 cm (14 in).

3 For the grass effect around the cake board, roll out 260 g (9 oz) of green sugarpaste into a thin strip and texture heavily using the scourer. To make the grass effect longer as it edges the base of the cake, cut along the edge of the rolled out paste by pressing in repeatedly using the star piping tube. Lift and position around the cake on the cake board, cut away excess at the back and close completely using the scourer to disguise the join. Trim excess from around the edge.

4 Cover the top of the base cake as the board using 315 g (11 oz) of green sugarpaste, texturing the surface with the scourer and the piping tube. To cover the top of the cake, roll out the remaining green and cut a circle slightly larger than the top of the cake and texture as before, securing on top of the cake with a little edible glue.

5 Cut out circles from the cake surface for the worms using the small circle cutter and remove the paste. Fill the grass areas with brown trimmings and the brown covering with thinly rolled out black sugarpaste.

6 Make their heads first using 20 g (¾ oz) of pale pink modelling paste for each. Roll into oval shapes and indent their smiles with the circle cutter, indenting the corners using a cocktail stick. For their eyes, roll pea-sized oval shapes of white for each and press them flat. Stick in position with a tiny black circle for a pupil.

7 For their bodies, roll balls of pale pink, some slightly graduating in size and press down on each to flatten slightly. Stick in position with a little edible glue using rolled up kitchen paper to support whilst drying. For the worm on the top of the cake, push the lolly stick down through the body and then stick on a worm head. Using green trimmings cut a circle with the circle cutter, texture as before and then stick in position onto the top of his head, for his hat.

8 To make the apple core, roll the cream modelling paste into a fat sausage and then roll back and forth in the centre to indent, rounding off each end. Slice small slivers from the surface inside using a knife. For the skin, split the pale green modelling paste in half, roll into balls and then roll out each into a thin circle large enough to cover each end of the apple core. Stick in position and then indent holes for the stalk and calyx using the end of a paintbrush. Roll a tiny sausage of brown trimmings and stick into one end for the stalk.

110

tip

This cake would look great with caterpillars instead of worms. Simply change the colours, using black and yellow or orange alternate balls of modelling paste or paint patterns over the surface using diluted food colouring and a fine paintbrush.

Apple core

The butterfly ball

What you will need

See pages 7 to 19 for recipes and techniques.

- 20 cm (8 in) round cake
- 450 g (1 lb/2 c) cake filling
- Icing (powdered) sugar in a sugar shaker

Sugarpaste
- 1 kg (2 lb 3¼ oz) pale green

Flower Paste (Gum Paste)
- 75 g (2½ oz) pink
- 20 g (¾ oz) green
- 30 g (1 oz) white
- 75 g (2½ oz) black
- 5 g (just under ¼ oz) yellow

- Edible glue
- Black food colouring
- Bright pink, yellow and green powder food colouring

Equipment
- 30 cm (12 in) round cake board
- Large rolling pin
- Small plain bladed knife
- Serrated carving knife
- Palette knife
- Cake smoother
- Butterfly cutters or templates (see page 127)
- 3 x thin 20-30 cm (6-8 in) lengths of food safe dowelling or skewers
- Daisy cutter
- Daisy calyx cutter
- Ball or bone tool
- A few cocktail sticks
- No.2 sable paintbrush (for edible glue)
- No.6 sable paintbrush or flat ended dusting brush
- No.0 (fine) sable paintbrush
- Small piece of voile net
- Food-safe foam sheet
- Miniature circle cutter or small piping tube
- 12 x food-safe black flower stamens

How gorgeous are these butterflies dancing together around a clump of daisies. With their cute faces and prettily painted wings this cake is sure to be a favourite.

Making the butterflies

1 Make the butterfly wings first. Thinly roll out the pink flower paste and cut out twelve wings using the template or butterfly cutters. As each wing is cut, smooth around the edge to thin out and then stroke vein lines over the surface using the paintbrush handle.

2 To make the stalks, cover the dowels or skewers with a thin layer of green sugarpaste. To cover, roll paste into a long thin sausage and place the dowel down onto the centre leaving some protruding at the bottom (this will be inserted into the cake). Using a little glue, wrap the paste around the skewer and then roll carefully back and forth to smooth the surface and close the join.

3 To make a daisy, thinly roll out white petal paste and cut two daisy shapes. Stroke down the centre of each petal to indent using a paintbrush handle, ball or bone tool. Stick one on top of the other and place onto the foam sheet. Press down into the centre of the flower with a ball tool, pushing gently into the foam sheet.

Indenting petals

4 For each flower centre roll a pea-sized ball of yellow modelling paste. Press the piece of voile net down onto the top to indent the pattern and flatten slightly. Stick in position.

5 For the butterfly bodies, split 30 g (1 oz) of black petal paste into six evenly sized pieces. Roll into long tapering teardrop shapes and curl up each end. Place each body on a foam sheet to dry with the curls overlapping the edge. Taking care not to break a fragile wing, press two wings down into the back of each body and then remove making slits for the wings to sit in later. If you prefer, make the slits with the template if used.

6 When the wings are completely dry, they are ready to be dusted with powder colours. Add the colour so each pair is slightly different and use the no.6 sable paintbrush or dusting brush. Dilute black food colouring paste with a few drops of water, diluting it enough to make a paintable consistency without being too watery. Paint the patterns over each wing keeping them symmetrical and once dry, turn over and repeat on the opposite sides.

7 Trim the crust from the cake and level the top. Cut layers in the cake and sandwich back together with cake filling, assembling on the centre of the cake board.

8 Using a sprinkling of icing (powdered) sugar, roll out the green sugarpaste to a thickness of 3-4 mm and cover the cake and cake board completely, smoothing down and around the shape. Use a cake smoother to gain a smooth dimple free surface. To smooth around the difficult to get at bottom edge of the cake, roll a 30 g (1 oz) ball of trimmings and rub gently over the surface, using as a cake smoother.

9 Push the daisy stalks down into the cake. Roll different lengths of green petal paste for grass and stroke along each length to indent. Stick in position supported by the stalks and grouped around the bottom of each.

10 To assemble the daisies, roll out green petal paste and cut out each daisy calyx. Thin out around the outside edge of each using the ball tool. Stick in position underneath a daisy and then stick onto the top of the stalk pushing gently down so the top of the dowel goes into the underside of the daisy and is held secure.

11 Stick the wings into the bodies of the butterflies and then stick in position around the cake using small pieces of foam sponge or rolled up kitchen paper to support in position whilst drying.

12 As their tummy area can flatten whilst drying, add a dome-shaped tummy patch to their fronts indenting along each by pressing in with the back of a knife. Carefully stick in position smoothing around the edge.

13 To make their heads, split 25 g (just over ¾ oz) of black and roll into ball shapes. Indent a smile using the miniature circle cutter pushed in at an upwards angle or use the end of a piping tube. Dimple the corners by pressing in with the tip of a cocktail stick. Stick in position and then add tiny oval-shaped noses.

14 Moisten each stamen and push gently into the top of their heads. Roll white ball shaped eyes and stick on small black pupils. For arms, roll thin sausages of black rounding off each end.

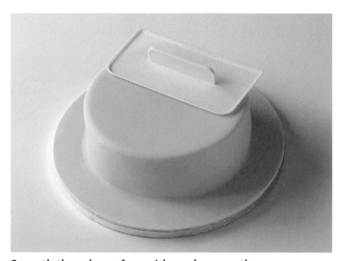

Smooth the cake surface with a cake smoother

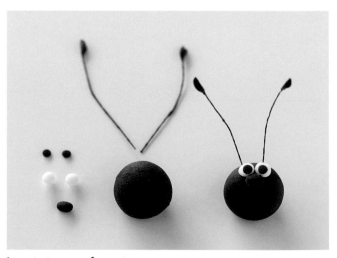

Insert stamens for antenna

114

Eyeballs

What you will need

See pages 7 to 19 for recipes and techniques.

- 1 x 15 cm (6 in) & 1 x 10 cm (4 in) square cakes
- 450 g (1 lb/2 c) cake filling
- Icing (powdered) sugar in a sugar shaker

Sugarpaste
- 1.25 kg (2 lb 12 oz) dark grey

Modelling paste
- 600 g (1 lb 5¼ oz) white
- 5 g (just under ¼ oz) green
- 5 g (just under ¼ oz) blue
- 5 g (just under ¼ oz) brown
- 5 g (just under ¼ oz) black
- 5 g (just under ¼ oz) red

- Edible glue

Equipment
- 25 cm (10 in) square cake board
- Large rolling pin
- Small plain bladed knife
- Serrated carving knife
- Palette knife
- A few cocktail sticks
- No.2 sable paintbrush (for edible glue)
- 2 cm (¾ in) circle cutter
- No.18 (PME) piping tube (to cut pupils)
- No.1 fine paintbrush
- Medium paintbrush
- Paint palette
- Brown and red flood colouring
- A few drops of cooled, boiled water
- Edible silver lustre powder
- Confectioners' varnish

This special collection of eyeballs seemingly hidden away in a deep dark cavern is certainly gruesome enough for any Halloween party, especially with all the blood red veins on show.

Gently press the sugarpaste covering against the cake

1 Trim the crust from each cake and level the tops. Cut a layer in each and then sandwich all layers and the two cakes together one on top of the other and position centrally on the cake board using a little cake filling to secure. Spread a layer of cake filling over the surface of the cake as a crumb coat and to help the sugarpaste stick.

2 Knead the grey sugarpaste until soft. Using a sprinkling of icing (powdered) sugar to prevent sticking, roll out and use to cover the cakes and board completely, smoothing down and around the shape. Stretch out pleats around the base and smooth downwards over the cake board. Pinch around the surface to make a rock effect and then trim away excess from around the cake board edge.

3 To make the eyeballs, split the white modelling paste into ten equal pieces and roll into balls. As the paste will be a little soft, roll each and then set aside until all complete and then go back and re-roll gently to gain a perfect ball shape.

4 Thinly roll out blue, green and brown modelling paste and cut circles for iris' using the circle cutter. Thinly roll out black and cut all the pupils using the piping tube (tip). Paint the detailing with the liquid brown food colouring using the step picture as a guide and then stick each in position.

5 Roll small thin sausages of red modelling paste for the veins, sticking in position on the back of each eye. Smooth the join outwards until level with the surface of the eyeball. Using red food colouring, paint the tiny thin vein lines.

Painting the iris

Brush glaze around the eyeballs to make them 'ooze'

6 To finish, brush a little edible silver lustre onto your fingertips and then rub over the surface of the cake to highlight the rock effect. Stick the eyeballs in position securing with a little edible glue. Using confectioners' varnish, paint a thin coat over each eyeball taking care with brush strokes so not to disturb the painted veins. Wait for a few moments and then paint another coat. Keep applying thin coats until a high shine is achieved. Brush a little confectioners' varnish around the eyeballs onto the cake surface.

Crowns and tiaras

What you will need

See pages 7 to 19 for recipes and techniques.

- 12 Cupcakes
- 175 g (6 oz/¾ c) cake filling
- Icing (powdered) sugar in a sugar shaker

Sugarpaste
- 450 g (1 lb) deep red

Modelling paste
- 315 g (11 oz) white

- Edible glue
- Silver and/or gold edible balls (dragees) or food-safe beading
- Edible silver and/or gold food colouring
- Edible or food-safe sparkle powder or glitter
- Edible sugar diamonds

Equipment
- Gold and/or silver 8 cm (3 in) thin round boards
- Gold and/or silver cupcake cases
- Large rolling pin
- Small plain bladed knife
- Serrated carving knife
- Palette knife
- A few cocktail sticks
- No.2 sable paintbrush (for edible glue)
- Kitchen paper

These gorgeous crowns and tiaras allow each little King and Queen or Prince and Princess to be presented with their very own special cake.

Use kitchen paper to support the crown frame

1 Spread a nice thick covering of cake filling to the top of six cupcakes making them dome shaped. Using 270 g (9½ oz) of red sugarpaste thinly roll out and cover each cake completely, stretching out pleats and smoothing downwards. Trim excess from around the base.

2 Cut different sized strips to decorate cut from thinly rolled out white modelling paste. For the crown frame, stick overlapping strips and support whilst drying with rolled up kitchen paper.

Add a little buttercream to the top of the cupcake to stick the cushion

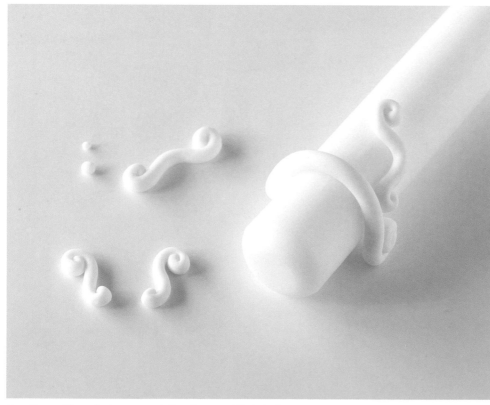

Use the rolling pin to support the shape whilst drying

3 Decorate with circles cut from the piping tube and indented circles. Paint either gold or silver. Add tiny red jewels by rolling ball shapes, stick on edible jewels and/or edible gold and silver balls or use beading.

4 For the cushions, thickly roll out red sugarpaste and cut 5 cm (2 in) squares. Soften the edge of each and then indent into the centre with your fingertip. Indent pleats using the paintbrush handle and stick a small red button on the centre.

5 Stick the cushions onto the top of the remaining cupcakes securing with a dab of cake filling. For the tassels cut tiny strips and pinch them together sticking in groups onto each corner with a small circle of red for the tie.

6 Make the bottom frame of each tiara using a 10 g (¼ oz) sausage of white modelling paste. Curl the ends around and secure with a little edible glue. Position this frame onto the rolling pin to dry. Make each tiara different by adding curled shapes to the frames and securing with glue.

7 When complete, brush the surface with a tiny amount of glue and then sprinkle the sparkle powder or food-safe glitter over the surface. When the tiara is completely dry, stand upright on a cushion and secure with edible glue.

Bugs

What you will need

See pages 7 to 19 for recipes and techniques.

- 12 x 6 cm (2½ in) bowl-shaped cakes
- 175 g (6 oz/¾ c) cake filling
- Icing (powdered) sugar in a sugar shaker

Sugarpaste
- 175 g (6 oz) blue
- 175 g (6 oz) lime green
- 175 g (6 oz) deep pink
- 175 g (6 oz) orange
- 175 g (6 oz) green
- 175 g (6 oz) yellow
- 90 g (3 oz) black
- 30 g (1 oz) white

- Edible glue

Equipment
- Rolling pin
- Small plain bladed knife
- Serrated carving knife
- Palette knife
- 6 x food-safe dowels or lolly sticks
- Small circle cutters (for smiles)
- A few cocktail sticks
- No.2 sable paintbrush (for edible glue)

Dotted around the party table these gorgeously gruesome, fun and colourful mini cakes decorated as bugs are sure to be a huge hit.

Preparing the bug's body

tip

If the cake filling is difficult to spread over the surface, dip the palette knife into hot water and then spread over the surface. The heat will make the surface smooth.

1 Sandwich two cakes with cake filling making a ball shape and then spread a layer over the surface as a crumb coat and to help the sugarpaste stick. Repeat for the remaining cakes. Leave the cakes to firm slightly before covering to help keep their shape.

The shapes required to build up the blue bug's face

Bug's bodies

2 To cover with sugarpaste, roll out to a thickness of 2–3 mm (⅛ in) and then cover the cake completely. Stretch out pleats and smooth downwards and around the shape tucking excess underneath. Roll the covered ball carefully in your hands to smooth the surface and then set aside. Cover all the cakes in the same way with their respective coloured sugarpaste.

3 Add tummy patches and/ or stripes by gently pressing the flattened shapes into the surface of the cake.

Bug's heads

4 Push a small dowel or lolly stick down through each cake ready for the head. Each head is either a ball or teardrop shape indented slightly in the centre using between 30–35 g (1–1¼ oz) of sugarpaste. Some heads have flattened circles for the neck.

5 For open mouths, push in with the end of a paintbrush and press downwards slightly. For smiles, indent with a circle cutter pushed in at an upwards angle. Smiles can be opened up slightly by brushing back and forth along the indented line with a paintbrush.

6 To make the blue bug's muzzle, roll a fat sausage back and forth at opposite ends to indent further rounding off the centre for the nose area. Curve the opposite ends round for the mouth and then stick in position over a small 'v' shaped bottom lip.

Bug's eyes

7 These are either white or coloured and some are edged with eyelids made with tiny tapering sausages of sugarpaste. For fun 'googly' eyes stick the pupils in position one higher than the other. To make eyelashes, roll tiny tapering sausages of black and use to edge between the eye and eyelid.

To finish

8 To complete the bugs, make tails with flattened circles of sugarpaste graduating in size. For the long feet, roll a thin sausage of sugarpaste, bend round half way and press flat for the foot.

9 To make antenna, roll tiny sausages of sugarpaste rounding off one end. Make a small hole in the bug's head ready for the antenna and stick in position when dry.

Templates

All templates are 100% actual size unless stated otherwise.

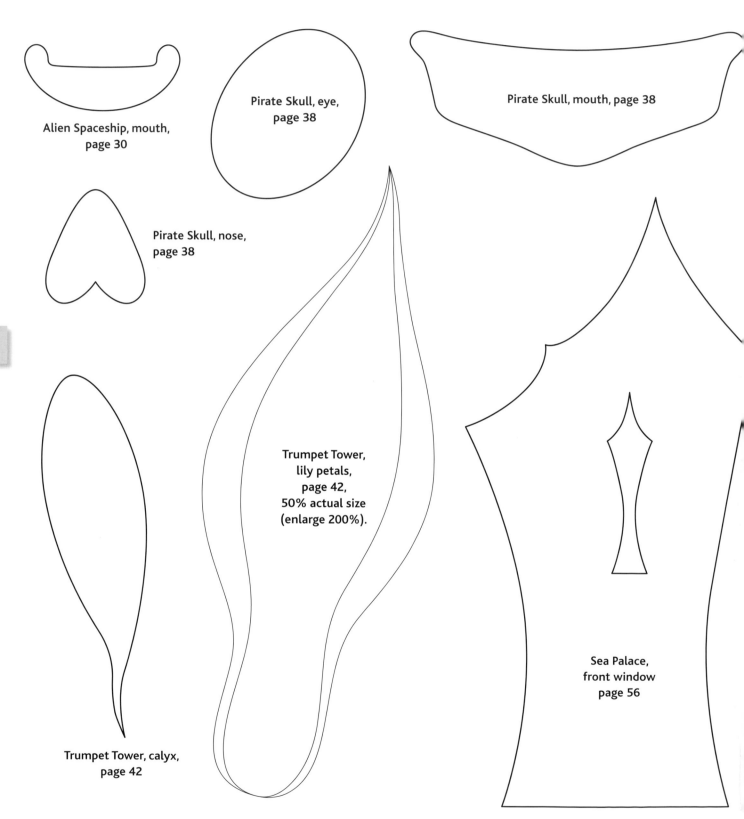

Alien Spaceship, mouth,
page 30

Pirate Skull, eye,
page 38

Pirate Skull, mouth, page 38

Pirate Skull, nose,
page 38

Trumpet Tower,
lily petals,
page 42,
50% actual size
(enlarge 200%).

Sea Palace,
front window
page 56

Trumpet Tower, calyx,
page 42

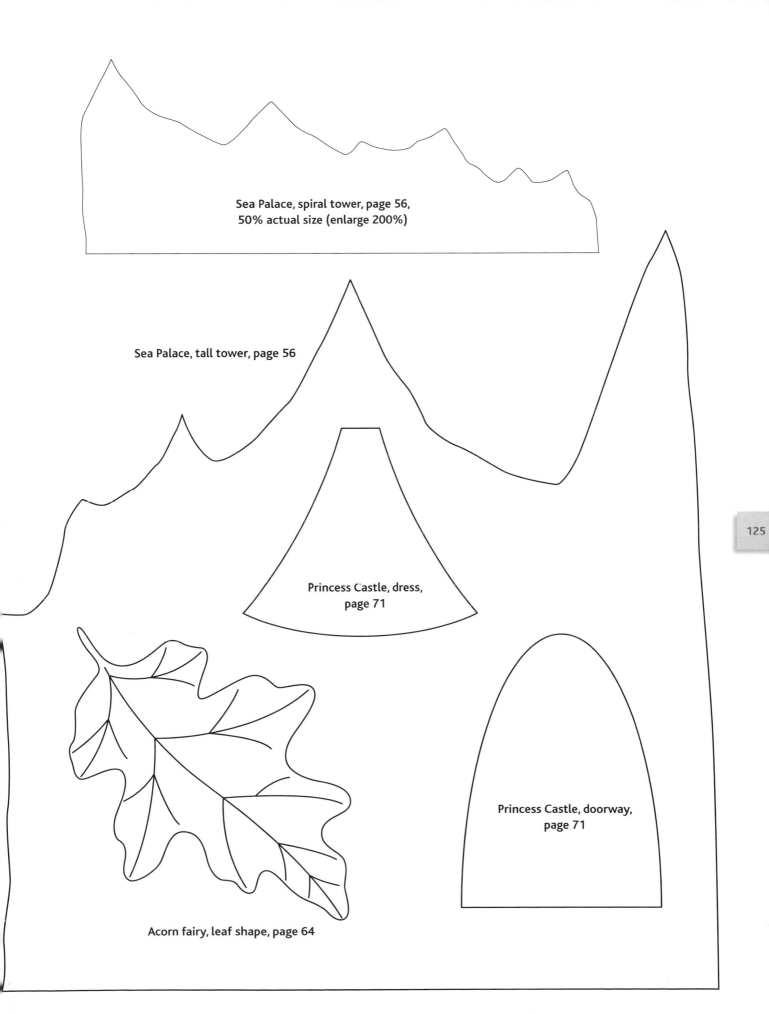

Sea Palace, spiral tower, page 56,
50% actual size (enlarge 200%)

Sea Palace, tall tower, page 56

Princess Castle, dress,
page 71

Princess Castle, doorway,
page 71

Acorn fairy, leaf shape, page 64

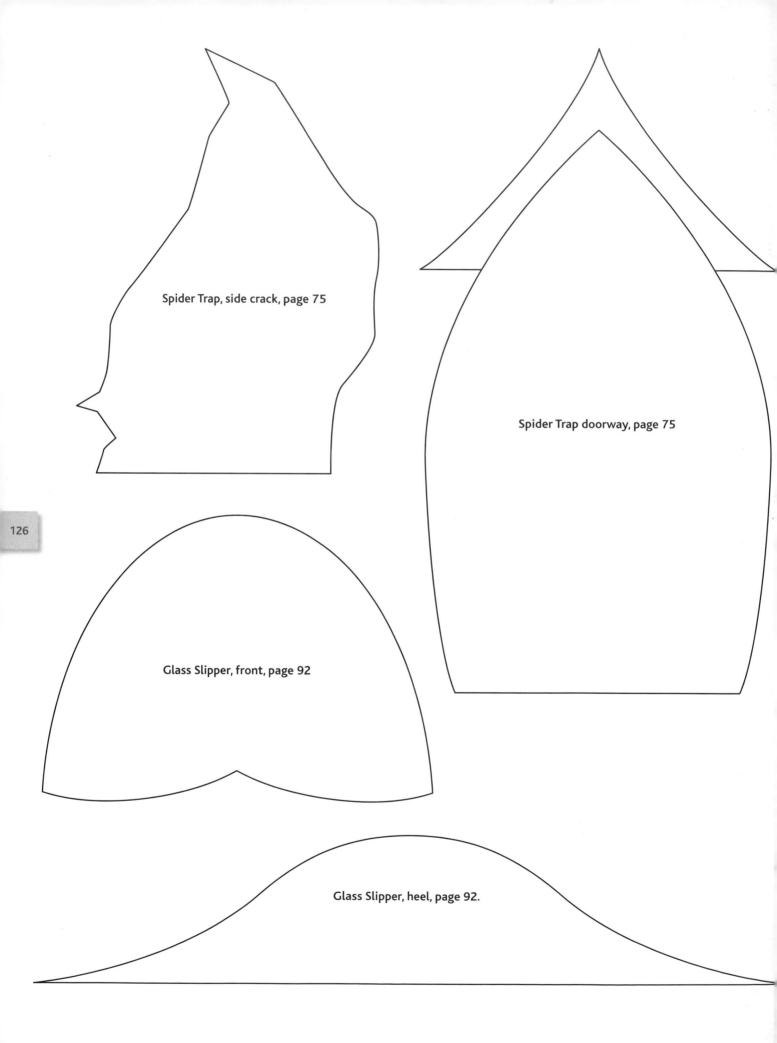

Spider Trap, side crack, page 75

Spider Trap doorway, page 75

Glass Slipper, front, page 92

Glass Slipper, heel, page 92.